The Neo-Thomists

Gerald A. McCool

MARQUETTE UNIVERSITY PRESS
MILWAUKEE

The Association of Jesuit University Presses

Marquette Studies in Philosophy

III

Andrew Tallon, Editor

Library of Congress Cataloging-in-Publication Data

McCool, Gerald A.
    The neo-Thomists / Gerald A. McCool.
        p. cm. — (Marquette studies in philosophy ; 3)
    Includes bibliographical references.
    ISBN 0-87462-601-3 (pbk. : alk. paper)
    1. Neo-Scholasticism. 2. Theology, Doctrinal—History—
19th century. 3. Theology, Doctrinal—History—20th century.
I. Title. II. Series: Marquette studies in philosophy ; #3.
B839.M395 1994
149' .91—dc20   94-42271

Printed in the United States of America
© Marquette University Press, 1994

Contents

Foreword

St. Anselm of Canterbury once described himself as someone with faith seeking understanding. In other words addressed to God he says "I long to understand in some degree thy truth, which my heart believes and loves. For I do not seek to understand that I may believe, but I believe in order to understand."

And this is what Christians have always inevitably said, either explicitly or implicitly. Christianity rests on faith, but it also has content. It teaches and proclaims a distinctive and challenging view of reality. It naturally encourages reflection. It is something to think about; something about which one might even have second thoughts.

But what have the greatest Christian thinkers said? And is it worth saying? Does it engage with modern problems? Does it provide us with a vision to live by? Does it make sense? Can it be preached? Is it believable? ...

In 1277 the Bishop of Paris (Stephen Tempier) condemned a number of propositions thought to be derived from the writings of Thomas Aquinas. The bishop's condemnation was ratified by the Pope of the day (John XXI) and by the Archbishop of Canterbury (Robert Kilwardby O.P.). But, as history has shown, Aquinas proved to be the most influential Christian theologian between St. Augustine and the twentieth century. In the SCM *Dictionary of Christian Theology* (London, 1983), he rates more references than anyone except Jesus of Nazareth.

Neo-Thomists are writers who stand within a tradition of thinking traceable (for various reasons) to that of Aquinas. Historians of ideas will disagree about the extent to which individual Neo-Thomists accurately interpret him.

And philosophers and theologians will differ in their judgments as to the worth of what they say. But nobody can deny that they have been a force to be reckoned with in Christian theological discussion, especially in Roman Catholic circles.

In what follows, readers will find a clear and concise survey of their thinking written by an acknowledged expert on it. There have been many books and articles written on particular Neo-Thomists. At the date of publication, however, Professor McCool's study is the only available English introduction to the full-range of Neo-Thomist writings. It should therefore prove of considerable value to students of nineteenth and twentieth century theology and philosophy.

Brian Davies O.P.

Chapter One
Thomism, Scholasticism, and Suarezianism

Leo XIII and the Revival of Aquinas

The term Neo-Thomism is generally employed to designate the movement in philosophy and theology which assumed a leading place in Catholic thought in the latter portion of the nineteenth century and retained its dominance until the middle of the twentieth. The philosophers and theologians associated with it were given the name Neo-Thomist, although, as we shall see, the name Neo-Scholastic might be a more accurate designation for some of them. Neo-Thomism could be considered a revival movement, since one of its major aims was the recovery of St. Thomas Aquinas's authentic thought. In its ambitions and achievements, however, Neo-Thomism was much more than a nineteenth century attempt to return to the Middle Ages. For Leo XIII (1810-1903), the Pope whose Encyclical, *Aeterni Patris* (1879), restored the philosophy of St. Thomas to a place of honor in the education of the Catholic clergy, was deeply immersed in the cultural, political, and social life of his own century, and it was on the basis of his understanding of the needs of his own time that Leo XIII became an advocate of a return to the philosophy and theology of the Angelic Doctor.[1]

Leo was convinced that, once it had been revived, the wisdom of St. Thomas could provide nineteenth century Catholics with the philosophical resources needed to integrate modern science and culture into a coherent whole under the light of their Christian faith. The Church's experience in the first half of the nineteenth century, Leo believed, had shown that modern Post-Cartesian philosophy could not provide her philosophers and theologians with the tools required for that important task. A new generation of Christian thinkers was needed equipped with more adequate philosophical resources. Only then could the representatives of Catholic tradition take their place in the community of contemporary intellectuals, and, through a lively exchange of views with its leaders, make an effective Catholic contribution to the intellectual life of Europe. St. Thomas was the philosopher to whom the Church should look for those resources. Through its link to the Fathers and the mediæval Doctors, the wisdom of St. Thomas could restore the bond between European thought and its Christian past which the Enlightenment and the French Revolution had severed, and restore to life the continent's intellectual and religious tradition. Furthermore, since, in Leo's eyes, the philosophy of St. Thomas was the most rigorous, coherent, and inclusive of the high mediæval systems, he was confident that it would measure up to the systematic exigencies of modern philosophy, while its openness to the Christian faith would keep it from falling victim to the religious and moral narrowness of modern thought.[2]

Clearly then the aim of the restorers of St. Thomas thought, as it express itself in Leo XIII's *Aeterni Patris*, was not restricted to the revival of a philosophy which modern Europe had practically forgotten. It envisioned the creation of a contemporary philosophy which, while taking its inspiration from the wisdom of the Angelic Doctor, would make its own contribution to the integration of European culture. To do that, the modern disciples of St. Thomas would have to learn a good deal from their heir colleagues of different philosophical persuasions. Philosophy, after all, had discovered many new truths and had corrected old errors in the centuries since St. Thomas' death. Yet, on the other hand, there were important truths which they could bring to the attention of their colleagues. For, in the two centuries since Descartes (1596-1650) had set philosophy on its new path, philosophy of knowledge, man, and being had moved away from the epistemology (theory of knowledge) and metaphysics of the Angelic Doctor. Yet it was precisely St. Thomas's epistemology and metaphysics which gave his system its remarkable coherence, inclusiveness, and rigor. A philosophy linked to the tradition of the Fathers and the great scholastic theologians and capable at the same time of working effectively in the nineteenth century intellectual milieu seemed, in the eyes of Leo XIII and of those who shared his vision, to be genuinely "perennial." At home in every age and culture, it was the philosophy which the universal Church should use for the education of her clergy.[3]

Thomism and Scholasticism.

Nevertheless, six full centuries had passed since St. Thomas's death in 1274 and Leo XIII's decision in 1879 to restore the Angelic Doctor to a place of honor in the education of the Catholic clergy. And for long periods during those centuries Thomas had been out of favor. Very soon after his death, in fact, several of Thomas's distinctive teachings were included on a list of condemned propositions issued in 1277 by Étienne Tempier, Bishop of Paris. Shortly afterwards Thomas's teaching was condemned again by his fellow Dominican, Robert Kilwardby, Archbishop of Canterbury. If Thomas had become a controversial figure at Paris and Oxford so soon after his death, it was clearly not the same thing to be a thirteenth-century scholastic theologian and to be a Thomist.[4]

The scholastic theologians, who taught at Paris and Oxford in the thirteenth century, received their name from their method of theological instruction. At Paris, and later at Oxford and Cologne, disputed issues were raised, discussed, and solved through the procedure of the *quaestio* or question. Following the custom of canon lawyers, the twelfth century theologian, Abelard (1079-1142), had extended to his own discipline the practice of grouping opposed authorities on either side of a clearly established "either-or" question. Once the existence of such a question had been determined, theologians, drawing on logic in the twelfth century, and on a fully developed philosophy in the thirteenth, could discuss it and solve it. In the school of a master of theology, students discussed such "disputed questions" before an invited audience of other masters. At a later session, their master resolved the question by proposing and defending his own solution. Finally, the published form of a *quaestio* ranged the opposed authorities on either side of the disputed issue, explained the principles on which the master's own solution were based, and answered the objections brought against it by the opposed authorities. Commentaries on Peter the Lombard's *Books of the Sentences*, composed in the form of a loosely linked series of questions, became an established form of thirteenth century theological instruction. Finally *Summas*, systematic expositions of the Catholic faith through a tightly woven set of questions structured by a single coherent system of philosophy, made their appearance.[5] Commitment to this common way of doing theology did not mean however that the thirteenth century scholastic theologians shared a common system of philosophy or that their views on the proper relation of philosophy to theology were identical. They did indeed draw on the philosophy of Aristotle (384-322 B.C.) for the shaping of their own theology. Nevertheless, they differed among themselves in their interpretation and adaptation of Aristotelian philosophy and in their general attitude toward its use in the structuring of Christian experience.

Plato, Aristotle, and the Theologians.

St. Thomas Aquinas (1224-74) was sent to Cologne as a young Dominican to study under St. Albert the Great (1206-80). He began his career as a "bachelor of the Sentences" lecturing on the four books of Peter the Lombard under the Dominican master, Elias Brunet, at Paris (1252-56).[6] In 1256 he succeeded Brunet as regent master of theology at the University and continued his work as a regent master at Paris, Orvieto, Rome, Viterbo and Naples until his death in 1274. The *corpus* of works which he left behind him is impressive in its size and diversity. It includes Thomas's early *Commentary on the Sentences*, his two *Summas*, the *Summa Contra Gentiles* and the *Summa Theologiae*, an extensive collection of special questions, a set of philosophical commentaries on Aristotle, Boethius (c. 480-c. 524), and Pseudo-Dionysius, the areopagite, a group of theological commentaries on the books of the Old and New Testament, and miscellaneous religious writings, such as prayers and sermons. Thomas's greatness however was not due to the size of his output, but to the inclusiveness and systematic coherence of the philosophical theology which he worked out to structure it.

Like the older theologians of his own order and his great Franciscan contemporary, St. Bonaventure (1217-74), Thomas drew extensively on the Christian Platonic heritage of St. Augustine (354-430). His master, Albert the Great, had introduced him to the second great stream of Christian Platonism, the theology of Pseudo-Dionysius and, like St. Bonaventure, he incorporated it into his own theology. Working in thirteenth century Paris, he had to face the same problem with which all the scholastic theologians had to cope. This was the challenge which the rediscovery of Aristotle's philosophy of knowledge, man, and being had posed to Catholic theology.

Plato (427-347 B.C.) had accounted for the mind's possession of its universal ideas through his celebrated theory of "recollection" or "reminiscence." According to this Platonic theory, at least as it was popularly understood, in addition to our temporal world of space and time, there was a higher eternal world. This was the world of the universal Forms which functioned as the changeless patterns after which the changeable realities of our lower world were fashioned—ideal equality, for example, or ideal justice. The Forms, in other words, were the pre-given "paradigms" or "models" which the concrete singular existents of our sensible world had to "copy" or "imitate" in order to be "what they were." Two logs in our world, for instance, could not be equal unless they "imitated" the perfect ideal Form of equality.

Before the human soul had "fallen" into its mortal body, it had lived a happy life "by itself" in Plato's ideal world; and, in that world, the soul had been able to contemplate the Forms directly. But its subsequent fall into our lower world had dimmed the soul's memory of its previous existence. Nevertheless, encounter in this life with the singular "imitations" of the Forms through sense experience could serve to "remind" the soul of their ideal paradigms. Thus, the soul's "reminiscence" of the Forms, which it had known in its previous existence, accounted for the origin of universal ideas in the human mind. Consequently, both the pre-existence of the soul and the extramental existence of a separate world of ideal Forms were the necessary conditions for the validity of Plato's account of conceptual knowledge.

Thus, when Aristotle denied the existence of Plato's separate world of ideal Forms, he was forced to come forward with a new explanation for the origin of universal concepts. The mind's knowledge of universal ideas would have to be derived from the sensible objects of our material world. For that to occur, however, the objects of our material world, known first through the organized sense image or "phantasm," would have to act, in some way or another, on the human mind. For, in the Aristotelian theory of knowledge, there was no place for anything like innate ideas. Before its content had been derived from sense experience, the Aristotelian mind could be no more than a "blank tablet"—a faculty endowed with an innate ability to know but completely devoid of any object capable of being known. Thus, until "something to be known" could be communicated to the mind by the operation of the senses, the mind itself could not perform its own intellectual act of knowledge.

In the technical language of his own philosophy, Aristotle compared the human mind before the reception of its content to the "primary matter" of his metaphysics. Aristotelian "primary matter" was the intrinsic constituent of a corporeal substance which could be called "real but not intelligible" because it had to be united to an intelligible "substantial form" in order to constitute a concrete "knowable substance." In an analogous way, the "blank tablet" of the human mind could be called "spiritual matter." For, until it had been "informed" by a content communicated to it by the senses, the mind had no intelligible "content" which it could know and possessed no "form" which could "determine" its amorphous power of knowing to know "this distinct object" or "that."

But how as Aristotle's amorphous "potential intellect" to receive such a concrete "form" or "content" from the determinate sensible singulars known through sense experience?

For, like Plato, Aristotle also held that the human mind was an essentially spiritual power of knowing; and, again like Plato, Aristotle held that the singular objects of sense experience belonged to the essentially lower level of material reality. Undeniably then the production of an intellectual idea in the spiritual mind exceeded the causal capacity of any material agent. At this point Aristotle found himself confronted with the classical difficulty which any philosopher who hopes to derive the content of intellectual knowledge from sense image, the production of the essentially higher reality of a spiritual idea.

Aristotle was the first philosopher to propose a plausible solution to that perennial problem — a solution which, in various forms, subsequent philosophers have continued to propose. In addition to man's "potential intellect," Aristotle explained, another cognitive agent of the spiritual order cooperated in the production of the universal idea. This second spiritual agent, he continued, was the "agent" or "active" intellect. The "agent intellect" did not itself perform the act of knowledge. Its function rather was to work in cooperation with the sense image or "phantasm" in the communication of the latter's content to the "potential intellect." Using the "phantasm" as its instrument, the "agent intellect" could then produce in the "potential intellect" the determined spiritual "form" which would enable that amorphous power of knowing to perform the determined act of "knowing this" or "knowing that." Under the influence of the "agent intellect," the content of the phantasm was dematerialized, and, as a consequence of its dematerialization, was de-individualized. The "dematerialization" of the content of the image, under the causal influence of the "agent intellect," was the famous "illumination of the phantasm." Its "illumination" raised the material content of the image to the spiritual level, and, by doing so, enabled a content, originally derived from sense experience, to "impress itself" on the "blank tablet" of man's "potential intellect."

"Abstraction" was the name given by Aristotelians to the whole process through which the content of a universal idea was derived from sense experience through the cooperative activity of the imagination and the "agent intellect." Aristotle's introduction of that spiritual elevating agent into his account of the origin of ideas enabled him to solve the classical problem connected with the derivation of spiritual ideas from the material content of sense experience; and, once Aristotle had solved that problem, Aristotelian abstraction became a viable alternative to Platonic reminiscence as an explanation for the origin of universal ideas.

In Plato's metaphysics the soul was a spiritual reality which had no need to be united to a body in order to exist or act. Indeed, the Platonic soul had been in a better state when it existed "by itself" in the ideal world of the Forms before the "fall" which had imprisoned it within the body. Escape from the body and return to its happier state of existence "by itself" in an immortal afterlife was the hope which a Platonic philosopher held out to a virtuous soul. For the Aristotelian philosopher, on the other hand, there could be no hope of an afterlife for the pure soul freed from the prison of its body since, in Aristotle's philosophy of man, the human soul was considered to be the substantial form of a living body.

In Aristotle's metaphysics every corporeal substance was a composite of primary matter and substantial form. Substantial form was the intrinsic constituent of a concrete corporeal substance which, by uniting itself to its material co-constituent, "determined" the concrete substance to be "what it was." Every concrete substance, in other words, owed its specific intelligible "essence" to the presence within it of its distinctive "substantial form." That singular form, on the other hand, was "individuated"—i.e. prevented from being a subsistent universal Platonic form—by the material co-constituent to which, in order to exist, it had to be united. Consequently, in Aristotle's metaphysics, neither primary matter nor substantial form were capable of existing by themselves. As co-constituents of the concrete existence substance, they could only exist in union with each other.

Thus, whereas in Plato's metaphysics, the intellectual soul could be considered an "independent substance" capable of existing and acting in separation from the body, the same could not be said of the intellectual soul in Aristotle's philosophy of man. For Aristotle indeed the intellectual soul, was a spiritual reality and its faculty of intellectual knowledge was the power of performing the intrinsically spiritual activity of rational thought. Nevertheless, that intellectual soul was the substantial form which communicated itself to primary matter to constitute the concrete human substance. The soul therefore was the animating principle of the living human body and, as a result, the soul itself was dependent upon its union with the body for its ability to perform its own operations. The activity of sense knowledge, for example, was an operation of both soul and body together in Aristotle's philosophy of knowledge whereas in Plato's philosophy of knowledge sensation had been an operation of the soul alone. Furthermore, in Aristotle's theory of cognition, even the purely spiritual activity of rational thought required the cooperation of the body. For, without the contribution of the sense image, human thought could have no object and, except through the medium of the sense image, the content of the mind's universal concepts could not be applied to the concrete realities of the material world.

Consequently the prospect of a happy afterlife for the soul freed from the body was dismissed as illusory by the followers of Aristotle. What happiness could there be for a separated soul which could neither sense nor think even if it continued to exist? But even continued existence without its body was impossible for the human intellectual soul. For, spiritual though it was, the intellectual soul was no more than the substantial form of a concrete living body. Consequently, it could not retain its own existence once its nature then the soul of man, in which his power of intellectual thought was rooted, was mortal. The spirituality required for intellectual activity could not therefore guarantee the immortality of the soul in which that spiritual power was lodged as Plato believed it did. The difference between the two philosophers therefore was not a difference about the spiritual nature of thought. It was a difference about the ori-

gin of ideas, and, partly as a consequence of that, about the
relation of the soul to the body.

Aristotle's metaphysics of knowledge, man, and being
therefore had important consequences for religion and ethics. The hope which Plato had entertained for an afterlife in
which virtue would have its reward and vice its punishment,
had to be abandoned. It is hardly surprising therefore that
the Fathers of the Church turned to Plato rather than to
Aristotle for their philosophy of knowledge, man, and God,
and that the theological tradition which came down to the
thirteenth century scholastic theologians was, to a large extent, the tradition of Christian Platonism.

By the thirteenth century the philosophy of Aristotle's
great "Arabian" Commentators, Avicebron (1020-70), and
Avicenna (980-1037)[7], had made its way to the Christian
West and the scholastic theologians began to adapt Aristotelian philosophy of knowledge and nature to the needs of
their own Augustinian tradition. Avicebron had already extended hylomorphism to the realm of spiritual reality and
devised a "universal hylomorphism" which could serve to
structure a Neo-Platonic participation metaphysics, and the
system of Avicenna too was a synthesis of Aristotelian and
Neo-Platonic elements. Scholastic theologians were able to
come to terms with the Aristotelianism of Avicebron and
Avicenna once the necessary modifications had been made
in it. A rather unsystematic blend of Neo-Platonized Aristotelianism and Augustine's Christian Platonic theology could
be worked out. Aristotle's "agent intellect" could be associated with the Augustinian metaphysics of divine illumination; through a plurality of substantial forms, Avicebron's
"universal hylomorphism" could serve the needs of an Augustinian participation metaphysics.[8]

Later in the thirteenth century however, Averroes (1126-
98), the greatest of the "Arabian" Commentators, began to
shape the philosophical instruction which future students of
theology received in the Faculty of Arts in Paris.[9] Much more
faithful to the text of Aristotle than Avicebron and Avicenna
had been, Averroes turned his back on the Neo-Platonic uni-

verse of emanation and participation. His world was an eternal and self-sufficient Aristotelian universe in which every movement in the world beneath the moon was determined with iron necessity by the revolutions of the heavens; and those revolutions in their turn were ruled with necessity by the intelligences which set them in motion. A single, immortal "active" or "agent" intellect accounted for the abstraction of universal ideas from the phantasms in the multitude of human imaginations. In Averroes's totally determined universe, there was no place for free will, and the human soul had no capacity for survival after its separation from the body. Platonic morality with its anticipation of sanctions in an afterlife, could not be reconciled with Averroes's coherent Aristotelian philosophy of nature, man, and God. Nor indeed could the Christian belief in a personal God who was the world's free creator and its provident guide. Once the Aristotelianism taught in the Faculty of Arts became the Aristotelianism of Averroes, the earlier accommodation between a Platonized Aristotelianism and scholastic theology in the tradition of St. Augustine was no longer possible. The attitude of the more conservative mediæval Augustinians toward Aristotle then become hostile. As St. Bonaventure put it, Aristotle, as a natural philosopher, might have "the word of science," but, as a metaphysician, he did not have "the word of wisdom." The world-view of Aristotelian philosophical science appeared to be incompatible with the world-view of Augustinian theological wisdom.

The Uniqueness of St. Thomas.

Thomas Aquinas however did not show the hostility to Aristotle which his more conservative colleagues displayed. Although he had been as firm as they had been in his opposition to the Aristotelianism of the disciples of Averroes at Paris, Thomas did not believe that Aristotle's philosophy of knowledge, man, and being was incompatible with a Christian theological wisdom. On the contrary, a fully developed theological wisdom could take the form of an Aristotelian science built upon the Aristotelian metaphysics of act and potency. To play that role however, act and potency could not longer be confined to the metaphysics of change explained through form and matter, as they had been in Aristotle's own philosophy. They would have to be transformed into a participation metaphysics. In that metaphysics, the primordial act would no longer be form, but the act of existence. Pure and infinite in God, the act of existence was limited in creatures by its correlative potential principle, the finite essence of each created participant. Once Aristotle's metaphysics of matter and form had been transformed into Thomas's participation metaphysics of essence and existence, it could expand its horizon to include the personal provident God whom Christians believed to be the world's creator; and it could do justice to the Platonic participation metaphysics of Augustine and Pseudo-Dionysius without recourse to the un-Aristotelian expedients of spiritual matter and a plurality of substantial forms.

Thomas himself gave a brilliant example of how a theological wisdom, structured by his expanded and corrected metaphysics of potency and act, could take the form of an Aristotelian science. In his theology of grace and nature, the sacraments, the human soul as the image of the Trinity, the creating and triune God, the angels and their knowledge, man's freedom and moral responsibility, he proposed a tightly woven synthesis of a nature and supernature, philosophy and theology. It was held together by a metaphysics of being, built around the act of existence, and a metaphysics of man as a dynamic Aristotelian nature, whose knowledge, beginning with sensible singulars, could ascend, by way of the analogy of being, to the infinite existence of God Himself.

Trained by his master, St. Albert the Great, in the negative theology of Pseudo-Dionysius, Thomas also inherited from Albert his uncompromisingly Aristotelian metaphysics of man and nature. Like every sensible singular, man was composed of pure matter linked immediately to a single substantial form.[10] The impact of Albert's fidelity to a single substantial form in the human essence on Thomas's participation metaphysics was powerful. Albert's Aristotelian matter, unlike the spiritual matter of Avicebron, had to confine itself to the realm of corporeal being, since the distinction between spiritual and corporeal matters required a plurality of substantial forms in the individual essence. If angels could no longer account for their finitude through a composition between substantial form and spiritual matter within their essence, the angelic essence must be a pure form limiting its participated act of existence.[11] As pure forms, angels could know themselves through immediate intuitive self-possession, but, as immaterial beings, incapable of being acted upon by other creatures, they could know other beings only through the intentional forms produced in them by their creator.

When man's intellectual soul was a substantial form received immediately in matter, the series of intermediate forms between the intellectual soul and matter, which the Augustinian scholastics required, could no longer be accepted. The immediate consequence of this was that anything like angelic self-possession by the intellectual soul became impossible. An Augustinian, or even a Bonaventurian, intuition of its own essence by the intellectual soul had to be excluded from St. Thomas's philosophy of knowledge. Yet, as Thomas argued against the Averroists, the human substance, composed of prime matter, spiritual form, and its act of existence, was a fully equipped and autonomous knower. Against the disciples of both Averroes and of Alexander of Aphrodisias (2nd century), Thomas argued that man was endowed not only with sense and imagination, but with his own active and passive intellects.[12] Man could know sensible reality, himself, and God. For, since Thomas's Aristotelian substance or nature had been created by God, the term of man's intellectual finality was no longer Aristotle's finite Prime Mover, but the Infinite God, the Pure Act of Existence. Thus, even though man was deprived of a vision of God through Augustinian illumination, the dynamism of his intellect enabled him to abstract universal concepts from singular images, posit the synthesis of universal and singular in the judgment, and mount from the contingent existents of the world of sense to their Infinite Creator. Aristotelian though his philosophy of knowledge might be, Thomas could ascend from sensible realities to God along the threefold path of affirmation, negation and eminence, which Pseudo-Dionysius had laid out in *The Divine Names*.[13] For, in Thomistic Aristotelianism, the ordering of the mind to Infinite Existence as its ultimate end served the function which *a priori* contact with the divine ideas served in the Augustinian metaphysics of divine illumination. It linked the mind to the whole realm of being.

Furthermore, Thomas's man was more than an autonomous Aristotelian nature. Man's mind, as Augustine and the Church Fathers had taught, was an expressed image of the Trinity. In Thomas's philosophical theology then the mind and will of man's autonomous human nature were ordered to the Triune God of Christian revelation as their unique, albeit supernatural, end. As were the angels, men too were ordered by the drive of their inborn intellectual appetite to an intuitive grasp of God in the Beatific Vision.[14] For all of that, the Aristotelian philosophy of knowledge, which Thomas used to underpin his account of the mind as the image of the Trinity, could no longer be the Augustinian philosophy which other Paris Doctors employed. With no intuitive grasp of his own essence, Thomas's knower could intuit no more than his own conscious operations. Nevertheless, his mind was not totally devoid of *intellectus*, or intellectual intuition. It could grasp an intelligible form in the sensible content of the image in what Bernard Lonergan has described as an act of direct understanding. Then it could formulate the content of that understood intelligibility in the mental word of the universal concept. Finally, through a reflective grasp of the justifying evidence, the mind could posit its synthesis of a universally formulated intelligibility and a singular subject in the unity of the judgment. Thus, in his radical revision of Augustine's trinitarian theology, Thomas created a new philosophy of knowledge in which immediate awareness of the operations of the mind, ordered directly to Infinite Existence as its end, linked knowledge of the singular to knowledge of the universal in the judgment and, with no reliance on Augustinian divine illumination, posited the synthesis of both in the world of real being.[15]

Once a created human nature became the expressed image of the Trinity, ordered, as the Fathers of the Church had taught, to the Triune God by its inborn dynamism, the order of Aristotelian nature could be given its proper place in the larger order of grace. And, even though Thomas's great contemporary, Bonaventure, refused to do so, Thomas could recognize Aristotle's metaphysics as an authentic wisdom ordering both human knowledge and its objects. When the finality of an Aristotelian human nature was linked to the Provident God of Augustine, the free creator who guided the finite agents in the world to their ends through his divine intellect and will, Aristotle's ethics of virtue and self-realization could be linked to Augustine's ethics of the eternal and natural laws and thus become a valid guide to human action. When the human knower's speculative knowledge of universal laws could be linked, as Thomas claimed, through the operations of his Aristotelian practical intellect, to the virtuous agent's individual acts, theoretical and practical moral knowledge could join hands to enlighten the experience of the religious man. The science of the theologian could be linked to the concrete experience of the prayerful Christian.

Thomas's original metaphysics, as we have seen, owed its origin to Albert the Great's fidelity to Aristotle. If, as Aristotle himself had said, there could be no more than a single substantial form in the concrete essence, the plurality of substantial forms proposed by the mediæval Augustinian theologians, by Bonaventure, and later by Duns Scotus (c. 1265-1308), could find no place in Thomas's philosophy of nature. And, since this excluded the explanation of participation through the limitation of form by spiritual matter proposed by the Augustinian scholastics, a new type of act and potency composition between the act of existence and its limiting essence was required. Thomas's philosophy of knowledge was also compelled to exclude anything like Bonaventure's linking of the agent intellect to divine illumination, since that linkage required a Bonaventurian intuition by the soul of its own essence. Furthermore, since Thomas's unitary substantial form was individuated immediately by prime matter, there could be no intellectual knowledge of the singular through intuitive grasp of its *haecceitas*, the last in the series of its formal constituents through which Scotus would claim that the concrete essence was determined in its individuality. Thomas therefore stood out in the ranks of the mediæval scholastics as a completely individual thinker whose rigorously coherent philosophy of being, man, and knowledge was peculiar to himself. The Augustinian scholastics knew that, and their hostility to Thomas's philosophy, and to the increased autonomy accorded to it in Thomas's theology, manifested itself in the condemnations of Thomas's teachings by Étienne Tempier and Robert Kilwardby in 1277.

The Sixteenth Century Revival of St. Thomas: The Second Scholasticism

Those condemnations cast a shadow on the philosophy and theology of St. Thomas and in the later middle ages it was never as popular as the theologies of Thomas's Franciscan rivals, Duns Scotus and William of Ockham (c. 1285-1347). A Dominican general chapter stood loyally behind Thomas in 1279 and his order made him its official doctor in 1313. Yet, even though Thomas found strong support among the fourteenth and fifteenth century Dominicans, and his cause was helped by his great commentator, John Capreolus (1380-1444), there were even some Dominicans who turned away from Thomas in search of another master.[16] As early as the turn of the fourteenth century, Durandus of Saint-Pourçain (c. 1275-1334), a Dominican theologian and future bishop, became on of the leading promoters of William of Ockham's nominalism, and in the fourteenth and fifteenth century other Dominicans gave their allegiance to Albert the Great rather than to Thomas Aquinas.

By the end of the middle ages anti-metaphysical nominalism had superseded both Thomism and Scotism and become the mainstream movement in scholastic theology. The resentment against scholastic theology which we find in *The Imitation of Christ*, the anti-intellectualist piety of the Brothers of the Common Life, and the open hostility toward the theology of the schools expressed by Renaissance humanists, like St. Thomas More (1478-1535) and Erasmus (c. 1469-1536) were all reactions against the arid formalism of the dominant nominalist theology. In the universities of the waning middle ages, St. Thomas's remarkable synthesis of philosophy and theology was no longer generally known.

By the turn of the sixteenth century however, the spiritual and intellectual revival of the Order of Preachers, with which the names of Savonarola (1452-98), and the two great Dominican generals, Cajetan (1469-1534) and Sylvester of Ferrara (1474-1528), have been associated was well underway. And, in the decades before the Council of Trent, Dominican theologians were able to make St. Thomas a leading authority once again in Catholic theology. Peter Crockaert (d.c. 1514), who became a Dominican at Paris, spearheaded the Thomistic revival at its University which influenced not only the Dominicans in France and Spain but, through St. Ignatius Loyola (d. 1556), who studied theology at the convent of Saint-Jacques at Paris after Crockaert's death, the Society of Jesus.[17] Although Crockaert's primary concern was with law and political philosophy, he appreciated the value of St. Thomas's ethics and metaphysics for Catholic social thought. In his school instruction, he replaced Peter the Lombard's *Books of the Sentences*, the standard textbook on which scholastics of all persuasions had commented since the thirteenth century, with Thomas's own *Summa Theologiae*. This radical innovation, soon to be imitated by Crockaert's Dominican colleagues in Spain and Italy, and, in a modified way, by Jesuit theologians as well, put Thomas at the very center of theological education. For the first time theology would be studied through the text of St. Thomas himself.[18]

Once that had occurred, new editions of St. Thomas's works and authoritative commentaries on them were needed. Crockaert himself brought out the first edition of the *Secunda Secundae* of Thomas's *Summa Theologiae* to be printed in northern Europe. In 1512 Conrad Köllin published a commentary on the *Prima Secundae*. Cajetan labored on his commentary on the whole *Summa Theologiae* and Sylvester of Ferrara followed suit with his commentary on Thomas's *Summa Contra Gentiles*. The age of the great teachers and commentators of the Thomistic Renaissance had begun. Crockaert's former student, Francisco de Vitoria (c. 1485-1546), became the first of a distinguished line of Dominican professors at Salamanca who made that university the center of a Thomistic revival in the Iberian peninsula. Vitoria's immediate successor was Melchior Cano, the author of *De Locis Theologicis*, the work which fixed the method of Post-Tridentine theology for centuries. Salamanca's influence extended beyond Spain and beyond the Dominican Order. Francisco de Toledo (1522-96), the Jesuit theologian and future cardinal, who had been educated at Salamanca, carried his Salamanca Thomism with him to the center of Jesuit higher education, the Roman College.

The devotion of the Society of Jesus to St. Thomas however, led to serious difference of opinion over what fidelity to Saint Thomas meant. In the Constitutions of his new order, St. Ignatius Loyola directed that Aristotle be followed as its authority in philosophy and St. Thomas as its authority in theology. Thus, in the early years of the order, Jesuit instruction in philosophy was based on the text of Aristotle and, to avoid Averroistic reading of the text, the Jesuit professors were obliged to make their own commentary on it. The most famous of their published commentaries was the four volume commentary on Aristotle's *Metaphysics* by Pedro da Fonseca (1528-99), the "Portuguese Aristotle," which became a standard work in both the Catholic and the Protestant universities of Europe.[19] Aristotle alone however failed to provide the foundation needed for Catholic theology, and the Jesuits found themselves obliged to prepare their own courses in philosophy. The most famous effort along these lines was the *Disputationes Metaphysicae* of Francisco Suárez (1548-1617) in which the greatest of the Jesuit theologians set forth the philosophy which underlay his own theology.

Suárez considered that St. Thomas was his master and that his own philosophy and theology, in all their essential positions, were a faithful continuation of St. Thomas's own thought. But, in his interpretation of Aquinas, Suárez was guided by the practice which Jesuit theologians employed in deciding which opinions they should follow. This was to choose the most common, approved, and secure doctrine. It was not a doctrine favorable to originality, and by following it, Suárez prevented himself from following St. Thomas in a number of the original positions, essential to his system, in which Thomas disagreed with the other scholastic doctors.[20]

The result was that, although Suárez agreed with Thomas about the unicity of substantial form and the rejection of anything like Augustinian illumination, Suarezian philosophy of knowledge and being drew on the thought of other scholastic doctors besides Aquinas. Suárez turned to Scotus to clarify the relation between the universal and the singular. Since our mind must know the singular, he reasoned, its knowledge cannot be confined to universal concepts abstracted from sense images. There must be some vague intellectual knowledge of the singular from which the universal can be abstracted through a subsequent act of precision. In his interpretation of Thomas's metaphysics, Suárez showed once more the influence of Scotus's epistemology. Thomas's distinction between essence and existence was reduced to a conceptual one; there was no act of existence, as the great Dominican theologians, Cajetan, Sylvester of Ferrara, and Domingo Bañez (1528-1604), claimed, really distinct from the essence which limited it. This meant, of course, that Thomas's Platonic participation metaphysics of act limited by potency was totally excised from Suarezian philosophy, and, in its Suarezian version, the philosophy of St. Thomas was portrayed as a Christianized Aristotelianism.[21]

The great revival of scholastic thought in the years after the Council of Trent has been called the second scholasticism. In the sixteenth and in the early years of the seventeenth centuries, a restored Scotism and the two rival interpretations of St. Thomas flourished in the Catholic schools of Spain, Italy and the German speaking lands. Suarezianism was taught in the extensive European network of Jesuit colleges and the Thomism of the great Dominican commenta-

tors, Cajetan and Sylvester of Ferrara, and of Dominican
theologians, such as Bañez and John of St. Thomas, was
taught not only in the Order of Preachers, but in the schools
of other orders, like the Discalced Carmelites and Bene-
dictines, in which adherents to the Thomistic interpretation
of St. Thomas could be found.

Thus, two influential "school traditions" in the interpretation of St. Thomas established themselves firmly in the seventeenth century. Suárez's *Disputationes Metaphysicae* had begun the tradition of replacing the commentary by a "course
in philosophy" for the instruction of future theologians. Then
the Dominican theologian, John of St. Thomas (1589-1644),
produced his influential Thomistic *cursus philosophicus* and
cursus theologicus. Courses in philosophy in the Thomistic and
the Suarezian tradition became common. Among them were
the widely used four volume Thomistic course by the seventeenth century Dominican, Antoine Goudin (c. 1639-95), and
another Thomistic course by the Discalced Carmelite, Philip
of the Holy Trinity (1603-71). Suarezian courses in philosophy were used in the multitude of Jesuit colleges.

But, by the second half of the eighteenth century, the
second scholasticism had gone into serious decline. The rise
of modern philosophy and the secularist spirit of the Enlightenment led to contempt for scholasticism among the educated elite, and the blend of Suarezianism and the rationalism of Wolff in the eighteenth century Jesuit courses in Philosophy, showed that even scholastics themselves were los-
ing confidence in their own systems. The disappearance of
the Jesuit colleges after the suppression of the order in 1772,
removed the tradition of St. Thomas in its Suarezian form
from its place in European education. The triumph of the
Enlightenment secularism and the attack on Catholic institutions after the French Revolution had practically the same
effect on the tradition of St. Thomas in its Thomistic form.

When the Catholic Church began to rebuild its shattered
educational system at the end of the Napoleonic Wars, both
had practically disappeared and, as a result of the eighteenth
century denigration of anything scholastic, even believing

Catholics knew scarcely anything about St. Thomas and saw little value in his thought. Thus, when Catholic theology began its slow recovery and was forced to meet the challenge of secular philosophy and culture, it turned to the more familiar Post-Cartesian or Post-Kantian forms of philosophy for its systematic framework. It was only after the publication of Leo XIII's Encyclical, *Aeterni Patris*, in 1879, that the second great revival of scholastic philosophy and theology, the "third scholasticism," became a force in Catholic education. In that revival of scholastic thought, both Suarezianism and Thomism returned to life in the Catholic schools and historical research began to recover the authentic thought of St. Thomas himself in its distinctive originality. It was in that movement of recovery, extension, and application of St. Thomas's thought, particularly in the twentieth century, that the Neo-Thomists made their appearance.

Notes

1. See Aubert, "Die Enzyklika 'Aeterni Patris' und die weiteren päpslichen Stellungnamen zur christlichen Philosophie" in *Christliche Philosophie im katholischen Denken des 19. und 20. Jahrhunderts*, eds. Emerich Coreth, S.J., Walter M. Neidl, and Georg Pfliegersdorffer, v. 2 (Graz: Styria, 1988), pp. 310-22.

2. For an English translation of *Aeterni Patris* see Jacques Maritain, *The Angelic Doctor: The Life and Thought of St. Thomas Aquinas*, trans. J.F. Scanlan (New York: Dial, 1931, pp. 224-62. Citations are to this edition. A second translation can be found in ed. Étienne Gilson (Garden City, N.Y.: Doubleday Image, 1954), pp. 31-54.

3. For Leo XIII's association with the revival of St. Thomas see Gerald A. McCool, S.J., *Nineteenth Century Scholasticism: The Search for a Unitary Method* (New York: Fordham University Press, 1989), pp. 226-40.

4. See James A. Weisheipl, O.P., *Friar Thomas D'Aquino: His Life, Thought, and Work* (Garden City, N.Y.: Doubleday, 1974), pp. 285-92; 331-43.

5. See Bernard J.F. Lonergan, S.J., "The Future of Thomism," in *A Second Collection*, eds. William A. Ryan, S.J. and Bernard J. Tyrrell, S.J. (Philadelphia: Westminster, 1974), pp. 45-49.

6. Possibly after a prior stay at Paris. See Weisheipl, *Friar Thomas D'Aquino*, p. 36.

7. In the thirteenth century Latin West the commentators who wrote in Arabic were assumed to be all Arab Muslims. In fact, Avicenna was Persian, and Avicebron, although he lived in Spain and wrote in Arabic, was Jewish.

8. See Fernand van Steenberghen, *Aristotle in the West: The Origins of Latin Aristotelianism*, trans. L. Johnston (Louvain: Nauwelaerts, 1955. Repr. New York: Humanities, 1970), pp. 159-62.

9. Averroes (1126-98) was born in Cordoba in Spain and died in Morocco.

10. For the hostile reaction to this teaching by the Franciscan theologians see Weisheipl, *Friar Thomas D'Aquino*, pp. 289-91.

11. See Thomas's *De Substantiis Separatis ad Fratrem Suum Reginaldum*.

12. In *De Unitate Intellectus contra Averroistas Parisienses*. For the background of this work see Weisheipl, *Friar Thomas D'Aquino*, pp. 272-80. See also Fernand van Steenberghen, *The Philosophical Movement in the Thirteenth Century* (Edinburgh: Nelson, 1955), pp. 75-93.

13. See Thomas's *Expositio super Dionysium De Divinis Nominibus*.

14. Following the tradition of the Fathers, Thomas held that the only end to which an intellectual nature was ordered by its creation was the supernatural end of the Beatific Vision. He did not hold, as later theologians, both Thomists and Suarezians, did, that there was a two-told finality in a created intellectual nature, a natural finality given to it by its creation, and a second supernatural finality added to the intellectual nature through a subsequent act of divine elevation. See Henri de Lubac, S.J., *Surnaturel* (Paris: Aubier,

1946). Even Thomists who were not particularly sympathetic to de Lubac, agreed that his interpretation of Thomas was correct. See Gerald Smith, S.J., "The Natural End of Man," *Proceedings of the American Catholic Philosophical Association* 23 [1949], 47-61.

15. The role of the act of insight in Thomas's original epistemology has been emphasized by Bernard J.F. Lonergan, S.J. in his study of Thomas's Trinitarian theology. See the large number of texts assembled and analyzed in Lonergan's *Verbum: Word and Idea in Aquinas* (Notre Dame, IN: University of Notre Dame Press, 1967).

16. For the support given Thomas by his Dominican brethren see Weisheipl, *Friar Thomas d'Aquino*, pp. 341-49. Half a century after his death Thomas was canonized in 1323.

17. Carolo Giacon, S.J., *La Seconda Scholastica*, 3 vols. (Milan: Bocca, 1946), v. 1, pp. 25-30.

18. Giacon, *Seconda Scholastica*, v. 1, 174-76.

19. See Ulrich G. Leinsle, "Die Scholastic der Neuzeit bis zur Aufklärung," in *Christliche Philosophie in katholischen Denken*, v. 2, p. 57.

20. For the influence of this practice on Jesuit philosophers and theologians including Suárez, see Charles Lohr, S.J. "Jesuit Aristotelianism and Sixteenth Century Metaphysics," in *PARADOSIS: Studies in Memory of Edwin A. Quain* (New York: Fordham University Press, 1976), pp. 203-20, esp. pp. 218-20.

21. For an extended account of Suárez's theory of knowledge see Eleutherio Elorduy, S.J. "El Concepto objectivo en Suárez," in *Pensiamento*, numero extraordinario [1948], 335-423. For Suárez's metaphysics see Juan Roig Gironella, S.J., "La synthesis metafisica de Suárez," *ibid.*, 169-213. English speaking readers can find a concise and accurate account of the Dominican Thomists and Suárez in Frederick Copleston, S.J., *A History of Philosophy*, v. 3 (Westminster, MD: Newman Press, 1953), pp. 335-405.

Chapter Two
The Nineteenth Century Revival

Opposition to the Revival of St. Thomas.

The Thomistic revival, which played a leading role in Catholic philosophy, theology, and social thought in the first half of this century, might not have occurred if Leo XIII had not become Pope in 1878. During the Catholic renaissance after the French Revolution, the philosophy taught in the Catholic schools of France, Belgium, and Italy was of two kinds. There was that associated with Felicite Robert de Lammennais (1782-1854), Joseph de Maistre (1752-1821), or Joseph de Bonald (1754-1840), whose characteristic thinking is sometimes called "traditionalism." This was a reaction to eighteenth century rationalism and it stressed the importance of faith as opposed to reason. Secondly, there was the approach associated with Vincenzo Gioberti (1801-1852) or Antonio Rosmini (1797-1855), commonly called "ontologism." This claimed its ancestry in the writings of Plato and Augustine and held that all human knowledge implies an immediate intuition of uncreated Truth (i.e. God). The resurgent Catholic theology in Germany during the first half of the century looked to Post-Kantian idealism rather than to traditional scholasticism for its philosophical resources. Even in the Society of Jesus (the Jesuits), after its restoration in 1814, scholastic philosophy did not make an immediate return, and, as late as 1850, the General of the Jesuits, John Roothan, complained to the Provincial of Lyons about the ontologism being taught to students of his Province.[1]

In 1824 Leo XII returned the Gregorian University, the venerable institution which had grown out of St. Ignatius's Roman College, to the Society of Jesus. The philosophers and theologians who taught there were orientated more in

the direction of traditional scholasticism than of the more
modern systems of philosophy and theology. Yet this did not
mean that they were interested in reviving the philosophy of
St. Thomas and making it normative for Catholic theology.
Giovanni Perrone, the best known Gregorian theologian in
the 1830s, felt none of the hostility toward modern German
theology which his fellow Jesuit, Joseph Kleutgen, would
display two decades later in his campaign to restore the philosophy and theology of St. Thomas, Later in the century,
Johannes Franzelin, a future cardinal, was the leading theologian at the Gregorian. Kleutgen and Franzelin were both
invited to work on the draft for Vatican I's constitution on
faith. But, whereas Kleutgen made the Church's teaching on
faith and reason one of the major arguments in favor of a
return to St. Thomas, Franzelin had little interest in a revival
of scholasticism. Like Newman, he did not wish to make
mediæval theology the norm for all theology. That might upset
the balance of Catholic theology, and it might diminish the
important role which the Fathers of the Church should play
in it.

The philosophers at the Gregorian were even less eager
to revive St. Thomas. Two of the best known among them at
the time when Leo XIII's *Aeterni Patris* was published were
Salvatore Tongiorgi and Domenico Palmieri. Both of them
were convinced that Aristotelian prime matter and substantial form could not be reconciled with the discoveries of modern science and that an Aristotelian philosophy of nature was
no longer viable. There were elements in mediæval metaphysics which still had a place in a modern system of philosophy
but St. Thomas's Aristotelian hylomorphism was not among
them. Any attempt to resurrect the Aristotelianism of the
Angelic Doctor could only be counter-productive.

Opposition to the revival of St. Thomas at the Gregorian
had begun as early as 1824. When the Jesuits reassumed the
direction of the University in that year, its young Rector, Luigi
Taparelli d'Azeglio, faced the problem which plagued seminary education at the time, lack of unity and coherence in its
philosophy program. Taparelli, who had become a convert

to the philosophy of St. Thomas, tried to solve the problem by basing the curriculum at the Gregorian on the philosophy of the Angelic Doctor. Stubborn resistance from the professors made that impossible. Five years later, as Jesuit Provincial of Naples, Taparelli, tried to make the teaching of St. Thomas the norm to be followed in philosophical instruction there. This time the reaction against his attempt to do so was so violent that it led to Taparelli's removal from office. In the beginning of the 1830s then it seemed that the attempt to revive the philosophy of St. Thomas in the Society of Jesus had ended in failure.[2]

The Dominicans and Naples.

In the Order of Preachers, on the other hand, despite the disruption of its intellectual life caused by the French Revolution, the tradition of St. Thomas had been preserved. Between 1777 and 1783, before the Revolution, the Neopolitan Dominican, Salvatore Roselli, published an influential Thomistic textbook, *Summa philosophiae ad mentem Angelici Doctoris Thomae Aquinatis,* which was used with great success for many years in Spain and Italy. The loyalty of the Neopolitan Dominicans helped to keep the tradition of St. Thomas alive there, and it is significant that, when the Neo-Scholastic revival began in nineteenth century Italy, the diocesan clergy of Naples provided some of its most influential leaders. The best known among them were Gaetano Sanseverino, Nunzio Signoriello, and Salvatore Talamo.

Ceferino González y Diaz Tuñon was the most influential of the Neo-Thomist pioneers in Spain. González had been a professor of philosophy at the Dominican University of Santo Tomás in Manila and Regent of the house of studies in Ocaña before his appointment as Bishop of Cordoba in 1875. In 1883 he was named Archbishop of Seville and, two years later, Cardinal Archbishop of Toledo, the Primatial See of Spain. Through his personal prestige, the influence he exercised on ecclesiastical education, and, above all, through his publications, González was able to bring the philosophy of St. Thomas back into Spanish seminary instruction. His

Estudios sobre la filosofia de S. Tomás and his three-volume text-book *Philosophia elementaria ad usum juventutis academicae ac praesertim ecclesiasticae* were widely read as was his briefer Spanish manual, *Filosofia elemental.*[3]

The most influential among the early Neo-Thomists in Italy were Tommaso Zigliara, whom Leo XIII was to make a cardinal, and Alberto Lepidi. Although Zigliara was Corsican by birth, his life as a Dominican was spent in Italy. As a young man he had won the confidence of the Bishop of Perugia, Giaocchino Pecci, the future Leo XIII. Pecci ordained the young Dominican to the priesthood and then appointed him to the faculty of his own diocesan seminary which he intended to make a center of Neo-Thomism. In 1870 Zigliara was appointed to the faculty of the Minerva, as the Dominican College of St. Thomas in Rome was popularly called, and in 1873 he was named its Regent of Studies. Zigliara's manual, *Summa philosophiae*, ran through seven editions and his more extensive three-volume text, *Summa philosophiae in usum scholarum*, was also widely used.

Before joining the faculty of the Minerva in 1885, Alberto Lepidi had taught for many years and served as Regent of Studies in the Dominican Convents at Louvain and at Flavigny in France. As Zigliara had also done, Lepidi took a critical view of ontologism in his *Examen philosophico-theologicum de ontologismo*, written at Louvain when ontologism was the dominant philosophy there. Again, like Zigliara, he was the author of an important Thomistic textbook, the three-volume *Elementa philosophiae christianae*. One of Ledidi's most lasting contributions to Neo-Thomism however was his reorganization of studies at Flavigny in his years as Regent there from 1868 to 1873. Revolutionary France had suppressed the Order of Preachers and it was not until the 1840s that, largely due to Jean Baptiste Henri Lacordaire (1802-61), the Dominicans were able to reestablish themselves. Lepidi helped to set the high intellectual standards in their philosophical formation which enabled the French Dominicans to play a leading role in the Neo-Thomistic movement.

In the twentieth century, French Dominicans would trace two different approaches to St. Thomas in their order back to Zigliara and Lepidi.[4] Zigliara stressed the Aristotelian elements in Thomas's philosophy and emphasized the dialectical rigor of his arguments. Lepidi, on the other hand, was drawn to the mystical side of Thomas's thought and was far more sympathetic than was Zigliara to the Augustinian and Platonic components in his philosophy.

The Jesuit Neo-Scholastics.

Thomas had also some disciples in Northern Europe. Mainz, for example, was a center of devotion to St. Thomas, and the Mainz review, *Der Katholik*, opened its pages to Joseph Kleutgen when he began his attack on the modern non-scholastic systems of philosophy. Mainz scholasticism could be traced back to the eighteenth century Jesuits in Strassbourg, and Mainz had no close connections with the Italian centers of the scholastic revival. Independently of Mainz, a few other German scholars, like Franz Jacob Clemens and Hermann Ernst Plassmann, had taken up the study of St. Thomas and argued for the revival of his philosophy.[5] But none of these isolated partisans of St. Thomas — not even the Dominicans or the diocesan priests of Naples — might have brought about a large-scale revival of St. Thomas were it not for the chain of events which began when two young seminarians began their studios at the Collegio Alberoni at Piacenza.

The college had been founded in 1751 by Giulio Cardinal Alberoni as a seminary for the diocesan clergy. The Italian Vincentians, who were its first professors, had a long tradition of devotion to St. Thomas and, even after their departure, St. Thomas was held in great esteem there. The most distinguished member of its faculty in the early years of the nineteenth century, Canon Vincenzo Buzzetti, was thoroughly Thomistic in his teaching.[6] The two young seminarians, Serafino and Domenico Sordi, were among Buzzetti's students, and, when they entered the Society of Jesus, they brought Buzzetti's enthusiasm for St. Thomas with them.[7]

In the novitiate, Serafino Sordi made a Thomist of his fellow-novice, Luigi Taparelli, and during his term as Rector of the Gregorian, Taparelli communicated his affection for St. Thomas to a promising young student, Giaocchino Pecci, the future Leo XIII. When Taparelli moved to Naples as Provincial he appointed Domenico Sordi to the faculty of the Jesuit philosophate. Sordi was no more successful than his Provincial in his effort to make Thomists out of the Neopolitan Jesuits, and, like Taparelli, he too was obliged to leave. Before his departure however, he did manage to influence two of his talented students, Carlo Maria Curci and Matteo Liberatore. And, at Modena, before he had come to Naples, he had made another young Jesuit a disciple of St. Thomas. This young scholastic was Giuseppe Pecci, the brother of the future Leo XIII and himself a future cardinal.

After 1850, the consequence of this fortuitous chain of events began to manifest themselves. Under Pope Pius IX the Roman reaction against the anticlerical policies of the European governments intensified, and, concerned over the confusion about the proper relations between faith and reason and nature and grace, Rome reacted against a number of non-scholastic theologies. Pius IX's first Encyclical, issued in 1846, defended the power of human reason both to recognize the credibility of revelation and to make a reasonable act of faith. Auguste Bonnetty's traditionalism was condemned in 1855; Anton Günther's theological works were placed on the Index in 1857: the theology of Jacob Frohschammer was condemned in 1862; and the ontologism of the Louvain philosopher, Casimir Ubaghs, met the same fate in 1866.

Furthermore, as a support for her influence in Italy, Pius IX wanted to found a review through which the Church could reach the Italian educated classes. Under pressure from the Vatican, the Jesuits agreed to staff it, and the review, *Civiltà cattolica*, began to be published in 1850. Carlo Maria Curci was its editor and Matteo Liberatore left his post as professor of philosophy at Naples to join its staff. About the same time, Joseph Kleutgen, a Jesuit Neo-Scholastic theologian, had established himself as the "German expert" for the Congregation of the Index. Kleutgen was known for his opposition to the newer German theologies and he would play an active part in the procedures which led to the condemnation of Anton Günther. Both Liberatore and Kleutgen thus found themselves well placed for the campaign which they would wage to replace the newer philosophies and theologies with the traditional scholasticism of which St. Thomas was the greatest representative.

In his early years as a professor of philosophy, Liberatore himself had been influenced by the more recent systems of philosophy. The first edition of his text book, *Institutiones logicae et metaphysicae*, published in 1840, makes that evident. The ten subsequent editions of the popular *Institutiones*, however, published in the two decades between 1840 and 1860, document a growing dominance of his thought by the Thomism which he had learned from Domenico Sordi and perhaps also from the Neopolitan Thomists. In any event, by 1853, Liberatore had become an ardent disciple of the Angelic Doctor.

In 1853 Liberatore began his series of articles in *Civiltà cattolica*. Brilliantly written and often polemical in tone, they presented a critique of nineteenth century philosophy, particularly of Italian ontologism, and an extensive exposition of St. Thomas's philosophy of knowledge, man, and being. The articles, which later appeared in book form as *Della conscenza intellectuale* and *Del composto umano*, together with Liberatore's *Istituzioni di Etica e Diretto naturale*, presented Thomistic epistemology, metaphysics, and ethics in the form of an integrated and coherent modern system of philosophy. As a system, Liberatore argued, the philosophy of St. Thomas was not merely equal to any of the post-Cartesian systems; it was superior to them.[8]

Between 1853 and 1870 the five volumes of Joseph Kleutgen's *Die Theologie der Vorzeit* also made their appearance. The five volumes mounted a persuasive argument in favor of Kleutgen's thesis that the nineteenth century Catholic theologies, whose philosophical framework had been taken over

from the philosophical systems of the modern age *(Neuzeit)*,
were not as well equipped to expound and defend the Catholic
faith as the older Scholastic theology employed by the Church
in pre-Enlightenment times *(Vorzeit)*. The problems which
the Church had experienced with her theologians in the nineteenth century had shown that their modern systems could
do justice neither to the distinction between faith and reason
nor to another important distinction connected with the first,
the distinction between nature and grace. Furthermore, the
post-Cartesian systems of philosophy, on which the modern
theologians relied, could not provide an adequate foundation for Catholic moral theology. For the evidence in support
of his position Kleutgen drew on his critical analysis of the
theologies of Georg Hermes (1775-1831), and the Tübingen
moral theologian, Johann Baptist Hirscher (1788-1865). The
aim of his critique was to show that the fundamental weakness of Catholic theology could be traced to its abandonment
of Aristotelian realism in epistemology, of Aristotelian act and
potency of its metaphysics of man and being, and of the Aristotelian scientific method which the scholastic theologians,
including St. Thomas, had employed. Then the remedy for
the weakness of nineteenth century theology became evident.
Return to the philosophy and to the Aristotelian scientific
method which characterized traditional scholastic theology,
die Theologie der Vorzeit.[9]

Kleutgen gave his exposition of that philosophy in the
two volumes of his *Die Philosophie der Vorzeit* which appeared
in 1863 and 1870.[10] Although Kleutgen and Liberatore had
worked independently of each other in their joint campaign
for the restoration of scholasticism, the similarity between
their philosophies is obvious. In their realistic epistemology
both reject the Cartesian doubt and the subjective starting
point which Descartes bequeathed to modern philosophy.
Human knowledge begins with sense experience. There are
no Cartesian innate ideas. Universals are acquired by abstraction from the phantasm. An Aristotelian realistic philosophy of knowledge, in which sense and intellect work together, demands an Aristotelian metaphysics of man and be-

ing in which there is no place for the Cartesian dualism between mind and body. On the contrary, man is a unified Aristotelian nature, a substance composed of prime matter and substantial form, from which man's faculties or powers of knowing and desiring are really distinct as its proper accidents. Thus, scholastic Aristotelianism shows that anything like an Augustinian or ontologist *a priori* intuition of God's necessary being is impossible. God's existence can be known only through *a posteriori* argumentation from the world of sense experience, and our analogous knowledge of God's essence is reached through the concepts abstracted from the sense images.

In the aggressive campaign which Liberatore and Kleutgen waged for the revival of St. Thomas, we see the mergence of *Neo*-Scholasticism. Written in the vernacular, Liberatore's articles and Kleutgen's books presented the philosophy and theology of the Angelic Doctor as a modern system ready and able to take on its revivals. The Neo-Scholastic system was also presented as the effective instrument which the Church required to cope with the problems which Rome considered to be the most serious ones with which she had to deal in the modern world: faith and reason, nature and grace, individual and social ethics. In the latter half of the nineteenth century that was a powerful argument for the revival of scholasticism at Rome.

It should be noted however, that it was for a revival of scholasticism rather than for a revival of Thomism that the two Jesuits were arguing. What they wanted to bring back to life was a philosophy and a scientific method which they considered to be the common property of all the mediæval scholastics and of their successors in the scholastic revival before and after the Council of Trent. Differences among the scholastics might exist, but they were not essential. They did not affect the fundamental of the unity of the philosophy, theology, and method shared by all and brought to its perfection by the Angelic Doctor.

In fact, both Liberatore and Kleutgen were Suarezians and they interpreted St. Thomas in the Suarezian way. No-

where in their metaphysics is there any place for the act of
existence, and in their epistemology the role of the act of affirmation, the intentional counterpart to the act of existence
in a Thomistic philosophy of the judgment, is overlooked.
Judgment for them consists in the union or separation of
two contents of knowledge, of two universal forms or of a
universal form with the singular which is its subject.

Aeterni Patris *and its Aftermath.*

In February 1878 Giaocchino Pecci became Pope under
the name of Leo XIII. The new pope had given clear signs
that he shared the conviction of Liberatore and Kleutgen that
the new systems of philosophy and theology were ineffective
and should be replaced by traditional scholasticism in the
education of the clergy. At Vatican I he had tried without
success to have the Council condemn ontologism, and in the
1850s he had made his diocesan seminary at Perugia one of
the most active centers of the scholastic revival in Italy. It
could be expected then that a pope linked closely to the leaders of the scholastic revival movement would encourage his
fellow bishops to follow the example which he had set in his
seminary at Perugia, and, in August 1879, he did precisely
that in his Encyclical, *Aeterni Patris.*

The proper distinction between faith and reason which
scholastic philosophy made possible, Leo wrote, could pre-
serve the distinction between philosophy and theology which
modern systems of philosophy often blurred. By preserving
that distinction, scholastic philosophy could mount strong
philosophical arguments for the credibility of revelation without compromising the transcendence of Christianity's revealed mysteries. When employed by the theologian, it could
organize the various parts of Catholic theology into an integrated, coherent whole; and it could provide the effective
arguments needed for controversy with the Church's enemies.
On its own strictly philosophical level, scholastic philosophy, which philosophized under the guidance of Christian
revelation, could direct human reason more surely than the

"separated" systems of modern philosophy which, on principle, ignored revelation in their philosophizing.

Those bishops then were to be commended who used for the education of their seminarians the sound scholastic philosophy of which the Angelic Doctor was the greatest representative. For in traditional scholastic philosophy and theology the Church's tradition was presented integrally and with systematic rigor. The Scholastic Doctors of the middle ages had gathered up the heritage of the Church Fathers, integrated it into a scientific system, and then bequeathed it to their successors. When scholastic philosophy was restored to life and returned to its proper place in the education of her clergy, it would provide the Church with a firm defense against the empiricism, rationalism, and skepticism which modern philosophy and modern science had spread among the educated classes. Historical research, of course, had an important part to play in that restoration, since the authentic teaching of the Scholastic Doctors must be distinguished from the distortions and accretions of later times. Contact between scholastic and modern philosophy should also be encouraged, since, in the development of a restored scholasticism, "every sagacious observation, every useful invention," no matter by whom it had been made, should be made welcome.[11]

On the whole, the reaction to *Aeterni Patris* by the Catholic bishops was favorable. Many of them had found the lack of coherence in seminary philosophy a vexing problem to which the Pope had now proposed a practical solution. In any case, Leo was determined to see that his program to revive scholasticism became effective. As a sign of things to come, he had made his bother, Giuseppe Pecci, and Tommaso Zigliara cardinals before the publication of *Aeterni Patris*, and Zigliara was also made prefect of the Congregation of Studies. Both Pecci, after his departure from the Society of Jesus, and Zigliara, had been on the seminary faculty at Perugia and both were known as partisans of the scholastic revival. After *Aeterni Patris* other signs of the Pope's intention to implement his program became visible. The Roman Academy of

St. Thomas was reactivated and Giovanni Cornaldi was appointed its director. Cornaldi was another member of the Jesuit group, associated with *Civiltà cattolica*, engaged in the campaign to replace modern philosophy with the scholasticism of the Angelic Doctor. At Leo's direction, the use of Cartesian manuals in the diocesan seminary at Rome was discontinued, and, at two Roman Universities, the Propaganda and the Appolinare, professors whose devotion to St. Thomas was suspect, lost their positions. Again, under pressure from Leo, a major shake-up took place at the Gregorian. Joseph Kleutgen was appointed Prefect of Studies and two of Kleutgen's stalwart opponents, Palmieri and Tongiorgi, were removed. When the Pope himself was a Neo-Scholastic, eager to bring about a revival of St. Thomas, the chances of that revival increased considerably.[12]

Mercier and Louvain.

Another important result of *Aeterni Patris* was the foundation of the Higher Institute of Philosophy at Louvain. Désiré Mercier (1851-1926) was teaching at the seminary at Malines when the Encyclical was published and, in 1883, he proposed to his Archbishop, Victor Cardinal Dechamps, that a chair in the philosophy of St. Thomas be established at Louvain. Leo XIII, who had been Papal Nuntio in Belgium before becoming Bishop of Perugia, expressed keen interest in the project, and when the Belgian bishops founded the chair in 1882, they designated Mercier to fill it. The Pope, as a sign of his pleasure at the choice, made Mercier a monsignor, and the latter began a long and successful career as a university lecturer. Five years later, in 1887, Mercier proposed that a Higher Institute of Philosophy be established at the University. In 1888 Leo XIII approved the project in a letter to the Belgian bishops. In 1889 the bishops gave their own approval and, at the Pope's request, named Mercier the director of the Institute. By 1893 Mercier was able to appoint as the first professors of the Institute four former students whom he had carefully prepared, and in 1894 the Institute's review, *La Revue néo-scholastique* made its first appearance. After some difficult negotiations, Rome agreed in 1900 to overlook Louvain's practice of teaching in the vernacular, although the other Pontifical Institutes were obliged to teach in Latin.

Mercier made a point of disinterested freedom in philosophical instruction and, living in anticlerical Belgium, he was conscious of the suspicion with which her positivist scientists regarded Catholic intellectuals. He was also aware of a renaissant scholasticism's need to learn more about its own past, and he realized that, if the disciples of St. Thomas were to interact successfully with modern philosophy, they would have to be well versed in its history. Therefore, modern science and history became the focus of attention at the Higher Institute. They shaped its curriculum as they had shaped the formation which Mercier had given to its founding professors. Simon Deploige (1868-1929) was a specialist in the social sciences; Maurice de Wulf (1867-1947) was an historian of mediæval philosophy; Désiré Nys (1859-1927) made his field the philosophy of the physical sciences; and Armand Thiéry (1868-1955) became a specialist in experimental psychology.[13]

Mercier chose epistemology as his own field of specialization, although he covered many other areas of philosophy in his lecture courses. His major work, *Critériologie générale ou Théorie de certitude*, defended the certitude of the intellect's universal and necessary judgments against the positivism of his day and what he took to be the subjectivism of Kant. This meant that, in a way, Mercier's *Critériologie* was very much a nineteenth century book. It looked back to the epistemologies of earlier nineteenth century Catholic philosophers, such as González and Tongiorgi, although it moved far beyond them; and, in its subjective interpretation of Kant, it followed the line taken by other nineteenth century Catholic interpreters.[14]

By the time that Mercier left Louvain in 1906 to become Cardinal Archbishop of Malines, the Institute of Higher Philosophy was firmly established and Louvain Thomism had put down strong roots. Louvain Thomism followed St. Tho-

mas rather than Suárez, and it was a university philosophy
in close touch with the contemporary sciences and the history of philosophy. Taught and written in the vernacular by
professors who had been students at other European universities, it was much less clerical in tone and less orientated
toward theology than the philosophy of other nineteenth century scholastics. With the inspiration and support of Leo XIII
Mercier had created at Louvain an independent and modern
Thomism.

The Roman Institutions

Unfortunately *Aeterni Patris* had quite different results at
Rome. With the departure of Palmieri and Tongiorgi, the
faculty of philosophy at the Gregorian became the base of a
new team of professors, Urraburu, De Maria, Schiffini and
Remer, whose commitment to the philosophy of the Angelic
Doctor was above suspicion. De Maria was a rigid and en-
thusiastic Thomist, and Remer's philosophical manuals, which
were used in seminaries throughout the world, became one
of the most effective channels for the transmission of Thomism in the closing years of the nineteenth century.

Often however the quality of the new professors at the
Gregorian and at the other Roman universities did not match
the quality of the professors whom they had replaced. The
professors at the Gregorian did not possess the originality
and breadth of the Neo-Scholastic pioneers Liberatore and
Kleutgen. Cornoldi, the only member of the new generation
of "Roman philosophers" who had any knowledge of modern science, shared their ignorance of modern philosophy and
was vehement in expressing his contempt for it. The publications of the Roman professors were basically school manuals whose purpose was the clear exposition of safe "received"
scholastic doctrine rather than the stimulation of original
thought.[15]

Neo-Scholasticism at the End of the Century.

In the two decades after *Aeterni Patris*, Neo-Scholastic
philosophy was largely a clerical enterprise. Many of its pub-

lications were Latin manuals which lay Catholics did not read
and to which the non-Catholic world paid no attention. As a
general term, Neo-Scholastic could be applied to Suarezians,
Thomists, and Scotists whose philosophical positions, more
often than not, were determined by the traditions of different religious orders. When the Society of Jesus "returned to
the Angelic Doctor" most Jesuits, although not all, did so as
Suarezians; and Franciscans could feel that Bonaventure and
Scotus, as Scholastic Doctors, were representatives of the
common scholastic tradition. The serious differences which
divided the mediæval scholastics would not be realized until
serious critical study of their texts made it evident. Neither
would the differences between St. Thomas's own thought and
the thought of his sixteenth and seventeenth century interpreters.

Nevertheless, the work of recovering the authentic
thought of the Angelic Doctor had begun. The Leonine Com-
mission, which Leo XIII established in 1880, started to prepare a critical edition of Thomas's works. Between 1882 and
1902, a team of Franciscan editors at Quaracchi near Flo-
rence brought out a definitive edition of St. Bonaventure's
corpus. Despite the deficiencies of these early editions, the
impetus which they gave to the critical editing of medieval
manuscripts was very great.

In 1880 two outstanding mediævalists, the Dominican,
Heinrich Denifle and the Jesuit, Franz Ehrle, were called to
Rome. Denifle was a Church historian whose specialty was
mediæval universities and mediæval mysticism. The discovery of Eckhardt's Latin works was due to him. Ehrle was a
specialist in the philosophy of the high middle ages and he
was the first to bring to light the conflict between the conservative mediæval Augustinians and St. Thomas Aquinas.
Denifle and Ehrle together founded the *Archiv für Literatur
und Kirchengeschichte*.[16] In Germany too, the serious critical
editing of mediæval manuscripts was under way. Although
Clemens Bäumker was not a Thomist in his own philosophy,
he recognized the distinctiveness and value of mediæval philosophy. In 1891 he founded the celebrated *Beiträge zur*

Geschichte der Philosophie des Mittelalters which he edited until his death in 1924. The high standards set by Bäumker's critical editing made the *Beiträge* the leading organ for the publication of mediæval texts and historical studies on mediæval philosophy. The history of mediæval philosophy, to which little attention had been paid, was now able to become an important and highly professional specialization.[17] Maurice de Wulf had begun his long and brilliant career at Louvain, and in 1899 the French Dominican, Pierre Mandonnet, brought out his epoch-making study on Siger of Brabant.

Interaction between Neo-Scholasticism and modern philosophy had begun in a serious way at the Higher Institute of Philosophy in Louvain. Yet, even there, as Mercier's *Critériologie* made evident, there was a long way to go. The Neo-Scholastic understanding of modern philosophy, particularly of Kant, was still deficient and the possibility of any reconciliation between St. Thomas's epistemology and the subjective starting point of post-Cartesian philosophy had not yet been considered. Neo-Scholasticism was still unknown, even by Catholics, beyond the world of the Church's own institutions. Yet the foundations had been laid for a remarkable development of the philosophy which *Aeterni Patris* had brought back to life. That development would occur in the twentieth century and, in the course of it, Neo-Thomism would distinguish itself clearly from the other forms of Neo-Scholasticism and, in its own evolution, would take on a number of diverse and distinctive forms.

Notes

1. Paul Gilbert, "Die dritte Scholastik in Frankreich" in *Christliche Philosophie im katholischen Denken*, v. 2, p. 416, n. 24.

2. See Thomas J. A. Hartley, *Thomistic Revival and the Modernist Era* (Toronto: University of St. Michael's College, 1971), p. 65.

3. For an account of González's philosophy see Carlos Valverde, "Ceferino González" (1831-1894) in *Christliche Philosophie*, v. 2, pp. 251-57. For González's epistemology see Georges van Riet, *L'Epistémologie thomiste* (Louvain: Editions de l'Institut Supérieur de Philosophie, 1946), pp. 107-11.

4. See Georges van Riet, *L'Epistémologie thomiste*, pp. 245-46. Van Riet cites Dominique-Marie Chenu's comment that unfortunately Zigliara's "Thomistic orthodoxy tinged with Wolffianism" had cut short the development of Lepidi's more profound Platonism among the French Dominicans. Nevertheless, Chenu believed that Lepidi's foundational work at Flavigny had shaped the intellectual tradition of the great twentieth century house of studies at Le Saulchoir.

5. See Peter Walter, "Die neuscholastische Philosophie im deutschsprachigen Raum" in *Christliche Philosophie*, v. 2, pp. 134-44.

6. See Giovanni F. Rossi, "Die Bedeutung des Collegio Alberoni für des Entstehung des Neuthomismus," in *Christliche Philosophie*, v. 2 pp. 82-108.

7. For Serafino Sordi's career see Paolo Dezza, *Alle origini del neotomismo italiaro* (Milan: Fratelli Bocca, 1940), pp. 29-64.

8. For Liberatore's philosophical system see Gerald A. McCool, S.J., *Catholic Theology in the Nineteenth Century: The Quest for a Unitary Method* (New York: Seabury, 1977), pp. 145-66. [Reprinted as *Nineteenth Century Scholasticism: The Quest for a Unitary Method* (New York: Fordham University Press, 1989)—same pagination].

9. For Kleutgen's theology See McCool, *Catholic Theology*, pp. 167-209.

10. For Kleutgen's philosophy see McCool, *Catholic Theology*, pp. 209-13.

11. For the text of *Aeterni Patris* see Jacques Maritain, *The Angelic Doctor*, pp. 224-62 or Étienne Gilson, ed., *The Pope Speaks to the Modern World*, pp. 31-54.

12. See Roger Aubert, *Aspects divers du néo-thomisme sous le pontificat de Léon XIII* (Rome: Edizione 5 Lune, 1961), pp. 30-31.

13. Georges van Riet, "Kardinal Désiré Mercier (1851-1926) und das philosophische Institut in Löwen" in *Christliche Philosophie*, v. 2, pp. 206-40.

14. Van Riet, *L'Epistémologie thomiste*, pp. 135-78.

15. Van Riet, *L'Epistémologie thomiste*, pp. 81-107.

16. Wolfgang Kluxen, "Die geschichtliche Erforschung der mittelalterlichen Philosophie und die Neuscholastik" in *Christliche Philosophie*, v. 2, pp. 367-68.

17. Kluxen, "geschichtliche Erforschung," pp. 368-72.

Chapter Three
Blondel, Bergson, and the French Dominicans

The Dominican Revival: Le Saulchoir.

By the close of the nineteenth century the neo-scholastic movement had made considerable progress, especially in
the religious orders and the ecclesiastical faculties, although
the Catholic laity as yet had not been much affected by it.
Under the direction of Msgr. Maurice d'Hulst (1841-96),
the Catholic Institute of Paris emerged as an important center of neo-scholastic thought in the early years of the twentieth century. Leading figures in the Neo-Thomist movement,
such as Émile Peillaube, Albert Farges, Antonin-Dalmace
Sertillanges, Ambroise Gardeil, and Pierre Rousselot, were
invited to teach there. The Jesuit Gregorian University at
Rome "had been made safe for scholasticism" by the vigorous intervention of Leo XIII. In Germany an internationally
known neo-scholastic philosopher, Tilmann Pesch, had
drawn attention to the Jesuit house of studies at Maria Laach
through his teaching and his writing. Pesch had founded the
influential review, *Stimmen aus Maria Laach* (later known as
Stimmen der Zeit) in 1879, and his Latin treatises on philosophy of man and nature in the *Philosophia Lacensis* series, written "according to the principles of St. Thomas," became standard textbooks in many European and American seminaries. The teaching and textbooks of the Jesuit professors of
philosophy and theology at Innsbruck, where seminarians
from many lands were educated, had restored Suarezianism
to Austria's Catholic University, and Innsbruck would remain a center of Suarezian philosophy and theology for the
first half of the twentieth century.[1]

More significant for the history of Neo-Thomism however, was the intellectual revival of the Order of Preachers,

notably in France. The Italian Dominicans, as we have seen, had a good deal to do with the survival of St. Thomas's thought in the eighteenth century, and two Dominican leaders of its nineteenth century revival, Zigliara and Lepidi, were later professors at the Minerva, the Dominican university in Rome, later known as the Angelicum. In the final decade of the nineteenth century, the faculties of philosophy and theology at the Swiss Catholic university at Fribourg were staffed by Dominican professors whose teaching followed the Dominican tradition of the Second Scholasticism. One of the first great historians of mediæval philosophy, Pierre Mandonnet, taught at Fribourg for twenty-six years before his departure for Paris in 1909. Gallus Manser, one of the leading German speaking Neo-Thomists, came to Fribourg's theology faculty as a diocesan seminarian in 1890, and, after entering the Dominicans, taught at the university for over forty years.

As early as 1862, after their reestablishment in France by Henri-Dominique Lacordaire, the Dominicans received ecclesiastical recognition for their house of studies at Saint-Maximin in the Maritime Alps. In 1865 a second Dominican house of studies was established at Flavigny near Dijon. Lepidi came down from Louvain in 1868 to serve as Flavigny's Regent of Studies and held that position until 1873. When the French anticlerical laws forced the Dominicans to leave Flavigny some years later, its faculties of philosophy and theology were able to remain in operation at Corbora in Corsica until the early years of the twentieth century. Then, in 1904, they were transferred to Le Saulchoir at Kain near Tournai under the direction of Ambroise Gardeil (1859-1931), who served as their Regent of Studies until 1911. They remained in Belgium until 1937 when the Dominicans of Le Saulchoir came home to France, settling in Étiolles in the Paris region.[2]

Le Saulchoir became an important center of French Neo-Thomism. Nearly all the French Dominicans prominent in twentieth century Neo-Thomism (Mandonnet [1858-1936], Gardeil [1895-1990], Sertillanges [1863-1943], Roland-Gosselin [1883-1934], Chenu [1883-1934], and Yves Congar [b. 1904]) at some time or other in their careers, were connected with this famous House of Studies. In their teaching and in their publications the Le Saulchoir Dominicans reflected in diverse ways the manifold strands of their common intellectual tradition, textual research, spirituality, and speculative development of the philosophical theology inherited from the great Thomists of the sixteenth and seventeenth centuries. The founder of Le Saulchoir, Ambroise Gardeil, had absorbed Lepidi's "Platonic Thomism" from his master, Reginald Beaudoin, whom Lepidi himself had formed at Flavigny. In the words of his former student, Garrigou-Lagrange, Gardeil was "a Thomist who loved to read St. Augustine and who liked to quote Pascal." But he was also a Thomist who had steeped himself thoroughly in the *Summa Theologiae*, and who had absorbed the metaphysics of knowledge, free will, and beatitude which Thomas had worked out in the *Summa's Pars Secunda*.[3] Thus, when Gardeil had to confront the problems concerning the freedom and rationality of faith which arose at the turn of the century, he looked for a resolution to them in St. Thomas's analysis of human acts in the *Secunda Secundae*. But, in the creation of his own speculative theology, he turned as well to the later Dominican theology of the act of faith. Applying his Dominican intellectual heritage to the problems of his own time through his books and articles on faith, apologetics, and spirituality, and through his articles and oral teaching on philosophical topics connected with them, Gardeil did more than address these contemporary problems. He laid the foundations for a twentieth century form of Neo-Thomism, which his student, Garrigou-Lagrange carried on, and toward which Jacques Maritain was sympathetic. Before considering Gardeil's own work however, something should be said about the intellectual and religious movements to which he was responding and about the problems which he was trying to solve.

Blondel and the Problem of Immanence.

At the close of the nineteenth century a reaction against empiricism and rationalism in France led to a renewed interest in religious thought. Although the state universities remained cool toward Catholicism, some firmly committed Catholics could be found among their professors. One of these was Louis Ollé-Laprune whose teaching influenced Maurice Blondel (1861-1949) in his student days at the École Normale Supérieure. The renewed interest in religion among French intellectuals, although encouraging to Catholics, was also a source of problems to their Church. For, in the late nineteenth century, religious thought did not always take forms which the current Catholic theology, still tinged with eighteenth century rationalism, found compatible.

Kantian and Post-Kantian philosophy had not had the great impact on theology in France which it had had in Germany, and Catholic theologians had not paid much attention to it. They were obliged to do so however after the Franco-Prussian War. At the war's close, the Protestant Faculty of Theology at Strassbourg moved to Paris. Its Dean, Auguste Sabatier (1839-1901), was a talented popular writer and, in the closing decades of the century, his publications made Schleiermacher's Liberal Protestant approach to faith and Christian Revelation readily accessible to educated readers. It was an approach with considerable appeal to intellectuals schooled in the Kantian and Post-Kantian idealism then popular in the French universities. For Schleiermacher (1768-1834), as for Kant, speculative reason could have no knowledge either of God or of the extra-mental world of "things in themselves." Philosophical proofs of a Revealing God's existence or of "revealed truths" guaranteed by signs and miracles could no longer be relied upon to justify a reasonable and morally responsible act of faith. The religious sentiment of a wholly immanent human consciousness then became the sole source of faith and the only norm of Christian Revelation. For Catholic theologians this was quite a challenge. If Schleiermacher was right, the apologetics and the theology of faith then being taught in the Catholic seminaries was no longer valid.[4]

Traditional theologians were not alone in recognizing the seriousness of the new challenge. Maurice Blondel had been convinced through his own experience at the École Normale Supérieure that idealism's first principle, the immanence of consciousness, was the major difficulty with which Catholics had to cope before they could convince educated unbelievers to accept the Catholic faith. Late nineteenth century idealists considered the historical "facts of Christian Revelation" proclaimed by its authentic witnesses as matters of no significance to them. Since man's interior life of consciousness required no knowledge of such external facts either for its intellectual or for its moral development, historical Revelation could be simply dismissed out of hand. Even if Christ had lived, and if the alleged witnesses of Revelation had told the truth, these were just external facts of history. They were no different from thousands of other singular facts which ancient historians could verify. Brute, singular, facts like these were completely "extraneous" to the vital needs of a consciousness whose immanent development must be directed by its own universal laws. On principle then, extrinsic historical facts, like the life of Christ or the preaching of St. Paul, could not be matters of concern either to the philosopher or to the philosophically enlightened intellectual. He had no need to know them. In fact, since they were useless distractions which might impede the progress of his inner life, he would be well advised to ignore them. The current Catholic apologetics had been devised to answer the arguments of eighteenth century Enlightenment philosophers who were willing to debate the claims of Christian Revelation. But late nineteenth century idealists had no intention of debating with Christian apologists. As a matter of principle, apologists were to be denied a hearing.[5]

At the end of the nineteenth century then Blondel found himself facing the same problem which had challenged Schleiermacher at its beginning. How can a point of entrance for Christian faith and Christian Revelation be found in a human consciousness locked inside its own immanence by Kantian critical idealism?[6] For no Kantian idealist would accept the claim of Cartesian or Wolffian rationalism that clear and distinct ideas, liked together according to the demands of a rigorous method, could become the bridge over which the mind could pass from its own immanence to the extramental world of infinite and finite being. Although Schleiermacher was a Protestant theologian and Blondel a Catholic philosopher, and although the solutions which each of them proposed to their common problem were different, Schleiermacher and Blondel were in agreement about the starting point from which any attempt at a solution to their common problem must set out. After Kant's critique of speculative metaphysics and its claims, the starting point could only be within consciousness itself.

Remaining strictly within the immanence of consciousness, a scientifically rigorous reflection on its dynamic movement must be able to show that the inner development of human consciousness, directed by its own universal laws, cannot achieve that inner perfection which the idealists claim to be its goal without a humble recognition of a personal God who transcends human consciousness and a corresponding openness to the revelation of His inner life which that personal God can make, should He freely choose to do so. In that case, the *possibility* of historical supernatural Revelation is *necessarily* demanded by the exigencies of consciousness's own immanent fulfillment. Thus an objection in principle against considering the claims of Revelation is shown to be without foundation. For what the Christian apologist claims is that the possibility of Revelation, manifested by the universal laws of consciousness itself, has been realized in fact. Far from requiring the philosopher to ignore the claims of Christian Revelation, his moral responsibility required the philosopher to examine them.

Blondel's case for a consciousness open to the possibility of historical Revelation was made in *L'Action*, the doctoral thesis which he defended brilliantly in 1893.[7] His philosophy of action was a dialectic of the "willing will," the spiritual dynamism whose built-in yearning would be satisfied by nothing short of the concrete God of Revelation. Blondel's Christian philosophy, which he termed a philosophy of exigence, traced the necessary dialectic of the "willing will" through an ascending order of the "willed will's" terms, the possible objects of man's concrete choices. Careful and honest reflection on the will's dialectic confronted the inquirer at its close with an unavoidable "free option." He could choose to open himself in reverent humility to a possible supernatural Revelation or he could deliberately refuse to do so. In the latter case, his negative "option" condemned him to utter frustration in his quest for life's meaning. No finite object in the world could satisfy the ineradicable longing of his "willing will," and unless the option to open himself to Revelation was made, he could never find the concrete personal God, the goal whose attraction gave meaning to the yearning of his will, and the Creator who, by sharing His reality with them, gave meaning to the objects of the finite universe.

Blondel's philosophy of action was directed against the "intellectualism" of nineteenth century rationalists who claimed that they could give a "complete explanation" of the universe in an abstract deductive system. With their eyes fixed on the abstract concepts of positive science or on the "ideas" of idealistic philosophy, they ignored the concrete volitional activity of the human subject. That is why they failed to find the God to whom it led. Action, Blondel insisted, could not be reduced to the "idea of action." The fatal error of the "intellectualists" was their failure to see that, unless abstract concepts and "ideas" were restored to their proper context in the dynamic action of the concrete subject and integrated in the light of it, reason could not find the truth. In a philosophy of action, leading to an unavoidable "free option," the concrete will, striving beyond all conceptual objects, and not the conceptual intellect, was the primary faculty of truth and being.[8]

In 1896 Blondel published his *Lettre sur les exigences de la pensée contemporaine en matière d'apologétique*.[9] The *Lettre* distinguished between an "extrinsic apologetics" built upon external justification of the authenticity of Christian Revelation through signs, miracles, and the historically verified credibility of its witnesses and an "intrinsic apologetics" directed toward man's inner desires and exigences. An effective contemporary apologetics, at least in its first stage, Blondel argued, should take the "intrinsic" form. Objective justifications of Christianity based on strictly intellectual arguments would have little effect. For the contemporary difficulties with Christian Revelation did not concern its reasonableness but rather its relevance to human life. The apologist could not answer those difficulties unless he could show that Revelation filled a void in human experience which nothing else could fill. Only then could modern man be expected to take the trouble to inquire into the reasonableness of accepting it. Furthermore, Blondel continued, we are not moved to make the act of faith by the intellect alone. The will and the dynamism of the spirit must make their own essential contribution to that act of free submission to God's authority. It followed then that, if the invitation to Christian faith was to be effective, it must not be addressed to the intellect alone, as it was in the current "extrinsic apologetics," but to the whole man.

In the years following the publication of Blondel's *Lettre* a lively — at times polemic — controversy took place between the Blondelians, particularly Lucien Laberthonnière (1860-1932), and the Dominican Neo-Thomists represented by Marie-Benoit Schwalm and Ambroise Gardeil. Laberthonnière was very critical of the Aristotelian metaphysics and the "extrinsic apologetics" of the neo-scholastic philosophers and theologians. Schwalm and Gardeil, on the other hand, defended both St. Thomas's metaphysics and the current "extrinsic apologetics' in a series of articles which, in their turn, were critical of Blondel.[10] Before examining these articles however, and their role in the development of Neo-Thomism, something should be said of another turn of the century philosophy which the Neo-Thomists considered to be both a stimulus and a threat to Catholic religious thought, the metaphysics of Henri Bergson.

Bergson: Intuition and Process Metaphysics.

As a genuine metaphysics and a philosophy of life, spirit, and mobility, Bergsonian philosophy was extremely attractive to a younger generation weary of arid positivism and its hostility to metaphysics. The world of positivism was a world of lifeless matter but, for Bergson (1859-1941), reality was the vital thrust of life and spirit, the *élan vital*. The upward thrust of the *élan vital* through the varied levels and forms of being accounted for the evolution of the universe. Science and the positivism which had made science its model were not in touch with the vital process of reality. For reality could not be grasped through the abstract concepts of the discursive intelligence. Reality was reached through the intuition of the metaphysicians, a form of knowledge more akin to instinct in some respects than to intelligence.

Under the influence of the will, the reflective spirit "bent back" upon its own ceaseless dynamic motion and, in doing so, grasped being in an immediate intuition. The concepts of the discursive intellect had no hold on being. Their function was purely practical. By dividing up the continuous process of the *élan vital* into static "bits and pieces," the concepts of the discursive intellect enabled thought to construct its logical enchainments. Man's practical intellect could then deal with his environment through the systematic deductions and reasonable anticipations of scientific thought. Conceptual intelligence, and its abstract mode of operation, accounted for the physico-mathematical method of the positive sciences. By breaking up reality's undivided flow into static "pieces," intelligence quantified it. By transposing the process or "time" of reality into discrete mathematical points and surfaces, intelligence transformed the flowing, divisionless "time" of the *élan vital* into static, divisible space. The fluidity of process was frozen into a plurality of static, quantified "things."

The utility of this transformation was unquestionable. Nevertheless the price paid for it was high. The spatialized world of positive science was a world of lifeless determinism. Whereas the real world, which revealed itself to intuition, was a world of spirit, process, freedom, and endless novelty, the scientific world of the intelligence was a world of material appearances linked to each other by logic and mathematics. In such a world there could be neither freedom nor novelty.[11]

In the early years of the twentieth century many young philosophers, including Jacques and Raissa Maritain, welcomed Bergsonian metaphysics. Maritain (1882-1973) never forgot that it was to Bergson that he owed his liberation from the despair to which the meaninglessness of a positivist universe had driven him. To these young philosophers, including many Catholics, Bergsonian metaphysics was the metaphysics which the times required. It challenged the imperialism of the conceptual intellect in science and modern philosophy. It was a metaphysics in which the real manifested itself in its true character as spirit, life, and process. The epistemological foundation for this new metaphysics was the Bergsonian intuition. Relativizing the intelligence by exposing its purely practical function, Bergsonian epistemology submitted conceptual knowledge to rigorous criticism and restored the intelligence to its proper — and secondary — place in the scale of knowledge. Philosophy had been opened once again to a world of freedom and self-development, a world of moral action in which, as many young Catholics thought, a free and personal God could reveal Himself. The timeless determinism of both positivism and rationalism had been overcome.

Problems with Blondelianism and Bergsonianism.

Blondelianism and Bergsonianism had many adherents among the educated Catholic laity and the younger clergy. They appeared to speak more meaningfully to the cultivated public than the desiccated philosophy and theology available in the seminary manuals of the period.[12] Both Blondel and Bergson knew nineteenth century university philosophy "from the inside" while most of the neo-scholastics did not, and their estimate of its possibilities and weaknesses were surer. On the debit side however, neither Blondel nor Bergson had a real understanding of the tradition of St. Thomas.

This was also true of their disciples. Either, as was the case of the laymen, they had no knowledge of it, or, as was the case with younger priests, they knew it only in the impoverished form found in their seminary textbooks. As a result, a fair amount of the controversy between the Blondelians and the Bergsonians on one side and the Neo-Thomists on the other, arose from mutual misunderstanding. For all of that, Blondelianism and Bergsonianism—usually as presented by imprudent disciples—turned out to be a source of serious problems for Catholic theology as became evident in the heat of the Modernist controversy.

How was Blondel's philosophy of immanence and exigence to be distinguished from a vaguely Schleiermachian conception of Revelation as a divine self-manifestation merging from the needs of human consciousness? And, if it could not be distinguished, what place remained for a distinctively Christian Revelation, given in history, and certified by the positive sources which gave witness to it? Furthermore, if concepts were valid only in the ongoing process of conscious action and, if, as Bergson claimed, they were of no more than practical value, what became of the speculative value which the Church assigned to her conceptually formulated dogmas? Were they no more than relative symbols whose value was to be determined by the practical needs of a religious experience grasped through non-conceptual intuition? Were dogmas then mutable, like the concepts through which they were framed, and should they be constantly revised to adjust to changing religious experience of the God found in consciousness and to the changing needs of the individual or the whole ecclesial community?

Bergson, who was not a Catholic, did not involve himself in theological controversies, and Blondel, who was a deeply religious Catholic, was angered at the implication that his philosophy threatened either the historical truth of Revelation or the abiding validity of Catholic dogma. A philosopher however cannot control the use of his name by others, and, in the early years of the century, George Tyrell (1861-1909), a leading Modernist, claimed to have been influenced by Blondel and the latter—most unjustly—was looked on with suspicion by some of his fellow-Catholics when the Church reacted strongly against what Roman authorities perceived to be the threat of Modernism.[13]

In reacting against Modernism and the relativization of
Catholic doctrine attributed to it, Rome renewed Leo XIII's
endorsement of the philosophy of St. Thomas. The epistemology and metaphysics of the Angelic Doctor were recom-
mended as a sure protection against the dangers of a philosophy of immanence, intuition, and process which had lent
support to the aberrations of the Modernists. St. Thomas's
epistemology of the concept and the judgment and his metaphysics of act, potency, and the analogy of being seemed to
provide the solid resources on which Catholic theology could
draw to insure its grasp on the immutable first principles of
being and the abiding validity of revealed truth.

Marie-Benôit Schwalm.

Blondel's problems with the Neo-Thomists however an-
tedated the Modernist crisis, and Blondel traced the origin
of the later misunderstanding of his philosophy, which caused
him so much trouble, to the extremely negative evaluation
of it by the Dominican Neo-Thomist, Marie-Benôit Schwalm
(1860-1908). Schwalm's article, "Les Illusions de l'idéalisme
et leurs dangers pour la foi" was published in the *Revue
Thomiste* in 1896.[14] Although conceding that Blondel's inten-
tions were orthodox, Schwalm claimed that the doctrine contained in *L'Action* and Blondel's *Lettre sur les exigences de la
pensée contemporaine en matière d'apologétique* was not. No fewer
than fifty statements of dubious orthodoxy could be found
in these two works. The source of these theological errors,
Schwalm believed, was Blondel's Kantian approach to philosophy. Post-Kantian idealism, which served as Blondel's
model, was a philosophy of immanence. This meant that it
was cut off both from the world of being and the normative
guidance of the teaching Church. Protestants might ignore
that teaching in their individualistic approach to faith, but at
least they acknowledged the Bible as faith's authoritative
norm. Idealists on the other hand would recognize no norm
beyond their own consciousness. This came down to saying
that every idealist could be his own Pope. How then could
idealism and Catholicism be compatible?

Schwalm's attack, which took Blondel by surprise, lacked measure and nuance. But, although it did not do justice to Blondel, it was the first expression of a negative attitude toward Blondel's philosophy which a number of Neo-Thomists would retain. Blondel had gone to considerable pains to distinguish between his *method* of immanence and a *philosophy* of immanence. In his *method* of immanence, Blondel explained, the starting point was within consciousness but the term to which its dialectic led, the Infinite God, was in the world of real being. In a *philosophy* of immanence, on the other hand, neither starting point nor term transcended consciousness. Schwalm ignored Blondel's distinction and simply treated Blondel as a Neo-Kantian idealist.[15] Later on, the Dominican Neo-Thomists, together with Maritain and Gilson, would understand the distinction clearly, but none of them would accept its validity. Their refusal to accept the validity of a starting point in consciousness distinguished the Dominican Neo-Thomists, Gilson, and Maritain from the Maréchalian Thomists. The latter accepted Blondel's contention that philosophy could begin its reflections inside of consciousness and work its way, through the dynamism of the mind, to the real being of God. Thus, by the second decade of the twentieth century, Neo-Thomists were divided into opposing camps over the attitude to be taken toward Blondel's philosophy of action.

In a personal letter to Schwalm, Blondel made another distinction which would be made again in the disputes between the different schools of Neo-Thomism. The misunderstanding between them, Blondel wrote, could be traced to Schwalm's tendency to extend the infallibility and immutability of defined dogma to the school metaphysics which the Dominican Thomists employed in their exposition of it. Granted that the dogmas themselves were infallible and immutable, it did not follow that Thomistic metaphysics shared the same characteristics. Dominican theologians, Blondel complained, were inclined to unit their own metaphysics to dogma in a way which he, as a philosopher, could not accept.[16] Fifty years later, in the controversy over the "New

Theology," the distinction between Thomistic metaphysics
and the immutability of dogma would be made again in the ex-
changes between the Jesuit Maréchalians, Henri Bouillard and
Jean-Marie Le Blond, and Dominican Thomists influenced by
Gardeil's former student, Reginald Garrigou-Lagrange.

Ambroise Gardeil.

Immanence, voluntarism, relativization of the concept
in favor of an immediate intuition of being, together with a
metaphysics of life and mobility rather than a stable metaphysics of being, these seemed to be the challenges which
the newer religious thought in France, stimulated by
Blondelianism and Bergsonianism presented to Catholic theology. They were made more acute by the popularity of William James's pragmatism and the prevalence of an inaccu-
rate interpretation of Newman's theology of faith.[17] Gardeil
was confident however that, in St. Thomas's metaphysics of
intellect and will and in the traditional Dominican theology
of the act of faith, he had found the resources needed to meet
the exigences of contemporary thought without running the
risk of doctrinal error.

He was well equipped to make the attempt himself since
he was an authority on theological method, known as an expert on the act of faith, and a Thomist respected for his grasp
of Aquinas's metaphysics of knowledge, will, love, and beatitude. Gardeil had been one of the pioneer editors of the
Revue Thomiste and his own teaching and writing was designed
to further that revue's program of historical recovery of St.
Thomas's own thought and exploitation of the possibilities
which it offered for the solution of contemporary problems.[18]

In 1898 and 1899 Gardeil published an important series
of articles in the *Revue Thomiste*. One of the aims of these
articles was to contrast the idealist immanence of consciousness with St. Thomas's metaphysics of the intellect and will.
In St. Thomas's metaphysics, Gardeil pointed out, human
knowledge was an immanent activity. Consequently, for the
Angelic Doctor as for the idealists, knowledge was a phe-
nomenon which occurred in consciousness. Nevertheless, St.

Thomas did not feel obliged, as did the idealists, to conclude that the immanence of consciousness required that its being be essentially diverse from the real being of "things in themselves." The idealists' "heterogeneity" between "conscious being" and "real being" did not exist in St. Thomas's metaphysics of consciousness. Thomas then had no reason to conclude, as Kant did, that "things in themselves" must be unknowable by their very nature. For Thomas, real being, including God's Absolute Being, was "metaphysically "homogeneous" with the being of consciousness. On the basis of that very homogeneity then, Thomas could show how the act of human knowledge, while remaining wholly immanent, could *transcend* consciousness and reach real being as its term. How did the metaphysics of St. Thomas make the transcendence of human knowledge within its very immanence possible?

Thomas's distinction between the faculties of the intellect and will, together with his metaphysics of causality, provided the answer. The intellect was a purely static faculty which grasped an object immanent in consciousness; on the contrary, the will, whose specifying object as a real being, a good which transcended consciousness, was a dynamic faculty. This was because, in St. Thomas's metaphysics of volition, God's Infinite Being was the Supreme Good, the Prime Mover which moved the will to act as the will's final cause.[20] Nevertheless, despite the diversity between God's Infinite Being and the essentially finite human consciousness, Infinite Being was not "heterogenous" to consciousness. It could not be, since the limited objects to which the will's appetite was directed were finite participations in Infinite Being. Thus Infinite Being became the conscious agent's *own good*. In this way the dynamism of the will, together with St. Thomas's metaphysics of participation, accounted for the fundamental homogeneity between consciousness and being which immanent and static human knowledge could not explain.

Even though St. Thomas taught that the will must tend toward a known good in its human acts, knowledge of the desired object was only a *condition* for the tending of the will toward it. For it was the *real good*, which transcends con-

sciousness, rather than a *known object*, immanent in consciousness, which drew the will toward it as the desired end.[21] But
how could such a real, and therefore, extramental, object
make itself present in consciousness in order to become a
known object? The answer, Gardeil explained, must be found
in St. Thomas's metaphysics of causality. If it is to be known,
the extramental object must first act upon consciousness. In
that case, the dynamic activity of the consciously willing agent
must be a *reaction* to the metaphysically prior action of real
being on it. Therefore, Gardeil continued, the ultimate solution of the problem of the immanence of consciousness cannot be reached on the level of consciousness itself, as Blondel
thought. The answer is found on the deeper level of St.
Thomas's realistic metaphysics in which both action and the
will's dynamic response to it are grounded in being—*agere
sequitur esse*.

In later articles[22] and in his book, *Le Donné révélé et la
théologie*[23] Gardeil revised his interpretation of St. Thomas's
metaphysics of knowledge and volition. He had come to see
that in St. Thomas's philosophy of man the intellect—and
not just the will—is a dynamic faculty. This did not lead him
however to follow the path of the Maréchalian Neo-Thomists
and ground the transcendence of human knowledge on God's
influence on the intellect as the final cause of its dynamism.
Gardeil believed that the necessary homogeneity between
consciousness and being was explained through the abstract
notion of being.[24] In St. Thomas's metaphysics, as he understood it, the dynamism of every human intellect contains
within it a virtually innate idea of being. When an external
object makes itself present to the mind and the intellect re-
sponds vitally to its activity, the transcendental concept of
being is formed in the mind's first act of abstraction. Then
the first principles of metaphysics flow immediately from this
abstracted concept. The idea of being then, contained virtually in the mind, is the light through which all reality—even
Infinite Reality—can be known.

Affirming an object under the light of being, the mind
becomes immediately present to itself. Then, as St. Thomas

explained in *De Veritate* I, 9, the mind, reflecting on its own activity, can know the goal of the natural finality which set it in motion. That goal, which is also the measure of the mind's activity, is being, present to the mind through its abstract and analogous concept.

Being, known through its analogous concept, is thus prior by nature to the mind's knowledge of its own activity. Therefore, the Cartesian "I think," which imprisons consciousness within its own immanence, is not the legitimate starting point for philosophy. On the contrary, Thomas's "Being is," which opens the mind to the whole range of reality, is the sound basis on which true philosophical reflection is built. Thomas's metaphysics of knowledge and direct, anti-idealistic realism go together.[25]

Through his reflections of knowledge and will in his *Revue Thomiste* articles, Gardeil intended to give a Thomistic reply to Bergsonian philosophy as well as a Thomistic response to an idealist philosophy of immanence. There were similarities between Bergsonianism and Thomism. St. Thomas agreed with Bergson that the human intellect possessed an immediate grasp of its own moving reality; and, as long as the term was understood in an imperfect and limited sense, that grasp could be called an intellectual intuition. But the differences between the two philosophers were also significant. For St. Thomas the mind's speculative knowledge both of its own and extramental being through the judgment rested on the first principles of knowledge and reality which flowed from the abstract and analogous concept of being. In St. Thomas's philosophy of knowledge, then, concepts had more than the purely practical value which Bergson was willing to concede to them. Concepts were the indispensable means through which the speculative intellect grasped being. Furthermore, in opposition to Bergson's metaphysics of pure mobility, the first mover of the mind and will was the Infinite Truth and Good, the motionless Pure Act of Being known to the intellect through the analogy grounded on the concept of being. Thus, Thomistic metaphysics gave a deeper and truer account of dynamic human experience than a

Bergsonian metaphysics of finite, self-grounding mobility in which no Infinite Mover set the intellect and will in motion.[26]

Thomas's metaphysics, in which being, known through the intellect, moved the will as its good, could correct the errors of contemporary exaggerated voluntarism in which the intellect was subordinated to the sheer dynamism of the will. It made little difference whether this contemporary voluntarism took the form of William James's pragmatism or of the Blondelian philosophy of action which its critics called neo-Scotism. Both suffered from the same defect, and the remedy for both could be found in St. Thomas's metaphysics of the intellect and will. The mind's reflection on its own dynamic motion, which Thomas had analyzed in *De Veritate*, I, 9, made it clear, through the objective evidence of being, present to the mind through its analogous concept, that the intellect — and not the will — was the faculty of truth. Thus it was to Thomas, rather than to Bergson or Blondel, that philosophers should look for the metaphysics of knowledge and volition which would enable them to break free from empiricism, rationalism, and Kantian idealism.

In opposition to Blondel's "intrinsic apologetics" Gardeil defended the "extrinsic apologetics" of signs and miracles and linked it to his own theology of faith.[27] His stand against Blondel was taken in a series of articles written in the *Revue Thomiste* between 1905 and 1907. In the following year Gardeil gave a full presentation of his apologetics and theology of faith in *La Crédibilité et L'Apologétique 28* and defended them again, in notably revised form, four years later in the second edition of that work.

Like his realistic epistemology, Gardeil's theology of faith was built upon a detailed analysis of St. Thomas's metaphysics of intellect and will. Both of these faculties were moved to action by God's influence of them as their final cause. The morally good agent, who must tend to God freely as his ultimate goal, could know God's existence by natural reason. He could understand as well that he was morally obliged to ascent to historical revelation should God decide to give it. Furthermore, the human mind could also establish the credibility of the historical revelation proposed to it through the signs and miracles which gave testimony to its authenticity. Nevertheless the Catholic Church taught solemnly that, without the aid of grace, no one could be justified through the free and supernatural act of faith. For this reason, in the revised version of his theology of faith, found in the second edition of *La Crédibilité et l'Apologétique*, Gardeil broke with the more common opinion favored by the Jesuit theologians. There could be no such thing, he now believed, as an act of "scientific faith," i.e. an assent to the credibility of revelation made by natural reason. Returning to the tradition of the older Dominican theologians he had come to hold that the judgment of credibility could only be made by a mind justified and elevated by grace as an integral part of the act of faith itself. Blondelian "action," in the form of a will tending freely under grace to its supernatural goal had found a place in Gardeil's "extrinsic apologetics."[29]

Gardeil returned to St. Thomas's epistemology of *intellectus*, intuitive self-knowledge, in *La Structure de l'âme et l'expérience mystique*, the great work on mystical theology written near the end of his career.[30] For St. Thomas the angels, as pure forms, know their essence exhaustively through an immediate act of *intellectus* or insight. Man, as a form received in matter, has no such exhaustive intuition of the soul which is his substantial form. Nevertheless the human mind, through *intellectus*, has an immediate awareness of its own activity in its knowledge of an extramental object. But, for St. Thomas the radical principle from which man's spiritual actions spring is his substantial form, the human soul. It follows then, Gardeil argued, that, since the human soul "comes to act" or "actualizes itself" in these spiritual actions, the mind's intuitive knowledge of them through *intellectus* is more than just an imperfect intuition of the actions themselves. Dim and imperfect though it may be, man's intuitive grasp of his own spiritual activity is a veiled and imperfect intuition by the soul of its own essential reality. In this quite radical interpretation of the epistemology of Thomas's *De Veritate*, the "Augustinian" character of Gardeil's Thomism revealed itself once more.

Marie-Dominique Roland-Gosselin.

In a series of articles published between 1910 and 1913, Gardeil's disciple, Marie-Dominique Roland-Gosselin, argued that Aristotle's theory of knowledge was the best to be found in classical Greek philosophy. By substituting abstraction of concepts from sense experience for Plato's direct intuition of the Forms, Aristotle was able to overcome rationalism without falling into empiricism; and, by making his abstracted idea of being the measure of the mind, he could secure the objectivity of knowledge while preserving its immanence.[31]

Post-Cartesian philosophy on the other hand, once it had rejected Aristotelian abstraction, was formed to vindicate the objectivity of knowledge through the mind's direct intuition of the real, and, as a consequence, it could no longer provide a satisfactory grounding for the analogy of being. Bergsonian intuition of moving spiritual reality was not the way to overcome rationalism and empiricism. More than intuitive self-knowledge was required to accomplish that. Concepts and judgments, ruled by the first principles of being, which flowed from its abstract concept, were also needed.[32]

In a number of articles published between 1913 and 1930, Roland-Gosselin took up St. Thomas's own theory of knowledge. Since, for Thomas, knowledge was a strictly immanent activity, an extramental object had to unit itself to the being of the intellect in order to be known. This union was effected by the *species*, the intentional nonmaterial form or similitude of the extramental object. Once the immaterial intellect had been brought from potency to act by the intentional form of the extramental object, it could perform its own immanent activity of known by "speaking" the "mental words" of the concept and the judgment. But, because the *species*, as an intentional similitude of the extramental object, was a relation, whose very nature was to refer the mind to an extramental object as its term in the act of knowledge, St. Thomas's act of knowledge transcended the immanence of consciousness.[33]

Although Roland-Gosselin did not believe, as his master did, that the soul had an imperfect intuition of its own essence, he agreed with St. Thomas that the mind had an immediate grasp of its own activity; and, like Gardeil, he held that through reflection on that activity, the mind could discover that the goal to which human knowing was directed was reality present to it through the abstract concept of being. The notion of being, as the *species*, or intentional similitude of all reality, was the light under which all reality, even the reality of the mind itself, could be known through the affirmation of the judgment.[34]

Following Gardeil, to whom his treatise on epistemology, *Essai d'une critique de la connaissance*,[35] was dedicated, Roland-Gosselin vindicated Neo-Thomism's epistemological realism both through his metaphysics of the *species* or intentional form, and through the role of the notion of being as the goal of the mind's activity. Realism was not justified through knowledge of the Divine Existence as the term of man's intellectual dynamism, as it would be in Transcendental Thomism. Neither could it be grounded on knowledge of the finite existence of the sensible singular, as would be claimed in Étienne Gilson's Existential Thomism (see below). For Neo-Thomism in the tradition of Gardeil, realism could not be grounded by the mind's grasp of existence, finite or infinite. It could be indicated only through the mind's knowledge of being as an essence — actual or possible — present to the intellect through the abstract concept of being.[36]

Réginald Garrigou-Lagrange.

As a student at Le Saulchoir, Garrigou-Lagrange (1877-1964) received a thorough grounding in the works of St. Thomas and of his great Dominican Commentators under the direction of Ambroise Gardeil. He remained at Le Saulchoir as professor of modern philosophy from 1905 to 1909, after which he was appointed to the faculty of the Angelicum, the Dominican university at Rome. Garrigou-Lagrange was a prolific author whose books and articles ranged widely over ascetical and mystical theology, revelation, apologetics, and the theologies of God and grace. His theological and spiritual writings, together with his exten-

sive expositions of Thomistic epistemology and metaphysics, won him an international reputation in Europe and in
both the Americas. Despite the variety of the topics on which
he wrote, the corpus of Garrigou-Lagrange reveals his clear
and coherent Thomism. It was also a stable and consistent
Thomism, for, although Garrigou-Lagrange continued to
write for four decades, his basic philosophical positions
changed very little.[37]

He made clear from the start that Thomas, interpreted
through the great Commentators of the Second Scholasticism, was his master; and, like Gardeil, he showed himself a
disciple of the classical Dominican theologians both in his
theology of faith and grace and in his manner of reconciling
divine activity and predestination with human freedom. This
set him at odds with the Jesuit apologists of the early twentieth century and brought him into conflict with the Molinism
and Suarezianism defended by a large number of Jesuit theologians until the middle of the century. Following Schwalm
and Gardeil, Garrigou-Lagrange also defended the "extrinsic apologetics" based on signs and miracles against the "intrinsic apologetics" favored by Blondel and Laberthonnière.
Again like Gardeil, he dismissed as invalid the "method of
immanence" in philosophy which Blondel had used in
L'Action.[38]

The starting point of his own philosophy was the mind's
immediate grasp of being and of the first principles which
flowed directly from its abstract concept. The use of Kant's
Transcendental Method was as unpalatable to him as the
"method of immanence" in philosophy associated with it. A
starting point in consciousness, of the sort employed by
Maréchalian Transcendental Thomism could not be reconciled with the evidence of being grasped immediately by the
mind through critical reflection on its own operation. Sound
philosophy, as St. Thomas had shown in *De Veritate*, I, 9, must
begin its reflection in the world of being.

Idealism, Blondelianism, and Bergsonianism were among
the major opponents against which Garrigou-Lagrange directed his Dominican Thomism. Bergson's disciple, Édouard

Le Roy (1870-1954) was the target of his first major work, *Le Sens Commun, la Philosophie de l'Être et les Formules Dogmatiques*.[39] Le Roy had argued that the genuine meaning of Catholic dogmas was the meaning given to them by common sense. Believing that, as a Bergsonian, Le Roy was tainted with Modernism and therefore denying the immutability of dogma, Garrigou-Lagrange determined to contrast what he considered the true philosophy of common sense found in the writings of Aristotle and St. Thomas with Le Roy's Bergsonian understanding of it. In St. Thomas's philosophy of knowledge, sense and intellect cooperate in the unitary act of human knowing. Therefore, common sense knowledge—the nontechnical knowledge of ordinary people unversed in philosophy—is genuine intellectual knowledge. In that case, common sense knowledge is ruled by the first principles which flow immediately from the abstract notion of being. In common sense, as in technical knowledge, being's stable self-identity manifests itself through the principle of self-identity or non-contradiction which rules every human judgment. From this it follows that the norm of true being must be its immutable actuality rather than the endless potentiality or "becoming" attributed to reality in Bergson's process metaphysics. The very failure of Bergson's "intuition of becoming" to reach the stability of being is a sign of its failure to reach the level of genuine intellectual knowledge. Restricted to the lower level of sensation, Bergsonianism can never be more than a refined empiricism.[40]

A year later, in 1910, Garrigou-Lagrange's article, "Dieu," appeared in the *Dictionnaire Apologétique de la Foi Catholique*. In 1914 the article was expanded into the well-known book, *Dieu: son Existence et sa Nature*, which later appeared in English as *God: His Existence and His Nature*.[41] A realistic epistemology, grounded upon Aristotelian abstraction and the mind's immediate grasp of being, allied to a metaphysics of act, potency, and the four causes, was the base on which Garrigou-Lagrange's defense of St. Thomas's proofs for God's existence was built. They were also the means through which St. Thomas could vindicate his claim that analogous knowl-

edge of God's attributes was possible. As Gardeil had done,
Garrigou-Lagrange insisted that the human mind could only
become aware of its own activity and of its natural ordination to being through its prior knowledge of a sensible singular. Bergson, on the contrary, had claimed that the mind's
primordial grasp of reality was reached through an intuition
of its own internal "becoming." But St. Thomas's reflection
on intuitive knowledge or *intellectus*, Garrigou-Lagrange con-
tended, had already shown the falsity of Bergson's assertion.
Man did indeed "understand" or "intuit" being through an
act of *intellectus*. Nevertheless, as Thomas had seen, this "intuition" occurred inside the larger process of Aristotelian
abstraction. Going beyond the level of sense in its act of intellectual knowledge, human *intellectus* intuitively grasped the
reality of being in the sensible singular at the very moment
at which the mind abstracted being's analogous concept. Far
from being a clear and distinct intuition of the knowing mind,
the "intellectual intuition" of being was a dim and confused
act of knowledge liked inseparably by its nature to the mind's
abstraction of being's concept from an external object of sense
experience.[42]

Two obvious conclusions followed immediately from this
discovery. First, the mind's intuitive grasp of being in the
sensible singular is prior by nature to the intellect's intuitive
awareness of its own "becoming." Second, without the prior
intuitive grasp of being in the sensible singular and the abstraction of being's concept associated with it, the reflecting
mind could not affirm the reality of its own intuited movement in a true and stable judgment. Consequently, Garrigou-
Lagrange argued, in one and the same reflection St. Thomas
had invalidated the claims of Bergsonian process metaphysics and Kantian immanentism through the evidence of being's
stable reality grasped immediately by the mind in the process of the judgment.[43]

For Garrigou-Lagrange, as it had been for the Dominican Thomists of the Second Scholasticism, and as it would
also be for Maritain (see below), the philosophy which took
its inspiration from St. Thomas was an Aristotelian science.

That meant that philosophy was ruled by Aristotle's meta-physics of act, potency, and the four causes.[44] It also meant that, in its treatment of philosophical problems, it should fol-low that order of exposition decreed by Aristotle himself: Logic, Natural Philosophy, Philosophical Psychology, Meta-physics, and Natural Theology. In Maréchal's Transcenden-tal Thomism, Epistemology would occupy the place of honor which Post-Cartesian philosophy had given it as the starting point of philosophical reflection. Taking their cue from the earlier Thomists, Garrigou-Lagrange and Maritain would make no such concession. For them the proper place for Epis-temology was in Metaphysics and the philosopher should approach it only after proper preparation through the study of sensation, intellection, and the immateriality of knowl-edge in Philosophical Psychology. As part of Metaphysics's reflection on being and its modes, Epistemology provided the philosopher with the reflective verification of being's first principles needed to appreciate St. Thomas's proofs for God's existence and to evaluate the knowledge of God's attributes which Thomas's analogy of being could give us.[45]

Being's necessary identify with itself, revealed in its simple concept, led immediately to the primordial principle of identity or non-contradiction; being is not non-being. Then it could be seen that the identity of being with non-being was not just unthinkable by the human mind, as the Bergsonians claimed; it was impossible in reality. And, in their proper order of priority, the other first principles flowed in their turn from the principle of identity: the principle of sufficient reason, the principle of efficient causality, the dis-tinction in being between accidents and the substances in which they have their sufficient reason, and ultimately the principle of finality.[46] Once he had a firm grasp on these first principles, the philosopher could mount from the contingent motion of the sensible universe through the rising levels of participated being along St. Thomas's five ways to God.[47] At their conclusion he found the efficient and final cause of the world's potential "becoming," the Infinite, Changeless Pure Act of Existence. Then, in his ultimate rejection of Bergson-

Bergsonianism, the philosopher had to affirm that, if the endless "becoming" of the finite world did not lead to Changeless Being as its origin and term, it led to absurdity.

Once the philosopher had broken free from the immanent world of the idealists and the moving world of Bergsonian process metaphysics, he could follow the path of being to St. Thomas's God. And, in a limited way at least, he could learn something of God's nature. Making use of the analogy of being, grounded upon the transcendental idea of being and St. Thomas's distinction between essence and existence, he could arrive at the indirect and imperfect understanding of God's attributes of which the human mind was capable.[48]

For Garrigou-Lagrange, as it had been for his great Dominican predecessors, a Thomistic philosophy, crowned by its metaphysics and theodicy, was to be used in the service of the higher science of theology. That theology, despite its dialogue with modern thought, remained the theology of the *Summa Theologiae* and the *Summa Contra Gentiles* read in the light of his inherited Dominican tradition.[49] This was particularly true of Garrigou-Lagrange's theology of grace, to which he assigned the central place in his theological synthesis.

Guided by the supernatural certainty of faith, Garrigou-Lagrange reach down through his apologetics and philosophy to the inquiring minds to which God manifested Himself first as the author of nature and then as the author of grace and revelation.[50] Then, with the Christian believer, he reflected upon the participation in God's intimate knowledge communicated through the gift of faith. Finally, after his scientific theology, Garrigou-Lagrange examined the experience of the Christian mystics and endeavored to explain it through the teaching of the Angelic Doctor. Taking his inspiration from the Carmelite Thomists of Salamanca, the Salmanticenses, and from Gardeil's theology of faith, he showed how the God, who made Himself present to the soul through the supernatural gifts of faith and the infused virtues, gradually withdrew His natural assistance to the senses, mind, and will in the passive purifications of the soul's dark nights, so that, at last, His supernatural splendor might reveal itself in its perfection.[51] Thus, for Garrigou-Lagrange, the wisdom of St. Thomas, the synthesis of his philosophy and theology, became the way in which the full range of Christian knowledge could be clarified and integrated.

The relation of scientific theology to lived spirituality was a matter of great concern to Garrigou-Lagrange. In addition to his courses in spirituality at the Angelicum and his treatise on St. John of the Cross,[52] he had published articles in the Dominican revue, *Vie Spirituelle*, practically from its foundation. His spiritual writing enjoyed great popularity, and, until the end of his life, he was in demand as a spiritual director. In this again he was following the tradition of the great Thomists of Second Scholasticism, some of whom, like Domingo Bañez, had united their teaching of scientific theology to the practical guidance of saintly souls.

Conclusion.

With Garrigou-Lagrange the tradition of Gardeil reached its full maturity. The elements of French Dominican Thomism were now in place: direct realism in epistemology grounded upon the notion of being as the immediate goal of the mind's dynamism; a philosophy of knowledge centered upon *intellectus* or intuitive self-awareness, the abstraction of the concept, and the intellectual intuition of being; an Aristotelian metaphysics of act and potency expanded to include the Thomistic distinction between essence and existence; a natural theology built upon the first principles which flowed from the transcendental notion of being and the analogy of being structured by the Thomists' distinction between essence and existence.

In its philosophy and its theology French Dominican Thomism looked back to the great Thomists of the Second Scholasticism and drew inspiration from the traditional Dominican theology of grace and faith. Its epistemology and metaphysics stood in opposition to both Blondel's method of immanence and to Bergson's philosophy of "becoming." Rather than embrace the "intrinsic apologetics" which Blondel and Laberthonnière promoted, Dominican Thomist apologetics relied on the "exterior" signs and miracles to establish the reasonableness of the act of faith confident in the support which its epistemology and natural theology could give to its arguments.

Thomism in the tradition of Gardeil was a distinctive form of Neo-Thomism. Being for it was defined as essence — actual or possible — made present to the mind through the abstract concept of being. It was not, as being would be for Gilson, the act of existence grasped in the judgment affirming the reality of a concrete sensible singular (see below). Neither Suarez nor the Maréchalian Transcendental Thomists were admitted to be authentic disciples of the Angelic Doctor. Thomism, in essence, was what the great Thomistic Commentators had said it was.

With the passage of time Garrigou-Lagrange found himself at odds with the historical approach to St. Thomas associated with Pierre Mandonnet, Maurice De Wulf, and, above all, with Étienne Gilson. After the Second World War it became clear that the St. Thomas of the great Commentators could not be reconciled with the historical Thomas of Étienne Gilson. The Thomism of Garrigou-Lagrange would also come into conflict with the Thomism of another distinguished historian, Marie-Dominique Chenu. Since Chenu was Regent of Studies at Le Saulchoir, that disagreement would lead to serious conflict within the Order of Preachers. The tradition of Mandonnet could no longer live in peace with the tradition of Gardeil.

Notes

1. Peter Walter, "Die neuscholastische Philosophie im deutschsprachigen Raum," in *Christliche Philosophie in katholischen Denken*, v. 2, pp. 178-82.

2. Paul Gilbert, "Die dritte Scholastik im Frankreich," in *Christliche Philosophie in katholischen Denken*, v. 2, pp. 423-29. For an excellent account of the history of Le Saulchoir see Marie-Dominique Chenu, O.P., *Une École de Théologie: Le Saulchoir* (Paris: Les Éditions du Cerf, 1985).

3. Réginald Garrigou-Lagrange, O.P., "Le P. A. Gardeil," *Revue Thomiste* 36 (1931), 800. See also H. D. Gardeil, *L'Oeuvre Théologique de P. Ambroise Gardeil*. (Étiolles: Le Saulchoir, 1956), and Van Riet, *L'Épistémologie Thomists*, pp. 244-46.

4. Roger Aubert, *Le Problème de l'Acte de Foi: Données Traditionnelles et Résultats des Controverses Récentes* (Louvain: Warny, 1950), pp. 267-77.

5. Aubert, *L'Acte de Foi*, pp. 274-82.

6. For Schleiermacher's theology see Brian A. Gerrish, "Friedrich Schleiermacher," in Ninian Smart, John Clayton, Patrick Sherry, Steven T. Katz [eds.], *Nineteenth Century Religious Thought in the West*. (Cambridge: Cambridge University Press, 1985), v. I, pp. 57-89. For an introduction and representative selection of texts see Keith W. Clements, *Schleiermacher: Pioneer of Modern Theology* (London: Collins, 1987).

7. Maurice Blondel, *L'Action: Essai d'une Critique de la Vie et d'une Science de la Pratique* (Paris: Alcan, 1892). Rev. ed. (Paris: Presses Universitaires de France, 1950). E.T. *Action: Essay on a Critique of Life and a Science of Practice* (Notre Dame, IN: University of Notre Dame Press, 1984).

8. For an excellent outline of Blondel's philosophy of action see James A. Somerville, "Maurice Blondel: 1861-1949," in *Thought* 36 (1961), 373-410. See also Somerville's book, *Total Commitment: Blondel's L'Action* (Washington: Corpus Books, 1963).

9. "Lettre sur les Exigences de la Pensée Contemporaine en Matière d'Apologétique et sur la Méthode de la Philosophie dans l'Étude du Problème Religieux," *Annales de Philosophie Chrétienne*; E.T. *The Letter on Apologetics and History and Dogma* (New York: Holt, Rinehart and Winston, 1964). Somerville's introduction to *Total Commitment* and the introduction to their introduction of Blondel's *Letter* by Alexander Dru and Dom Iltydd Trethowen are among the best introductions to Blondel to be found in English.

10. See Aubert, *L'Acte de Foi*, pp. 294-356.

11. For a clear and thorough account of Bergson's philosophy see Frederick Copleston, S.J., *A History of Philosophy* (London: Search Press, 1975), v. 11, pp. 178-215.

12. Étienne Gilson, *The Philosopher and Theology* (New York: Random House, 1962), pp. 106-31.

13. For a clear and balanced account of Modernism see Bernard M.G. Reardon, "Roman Catholic Modernism," in *Nineteenth Century Religious Thought in the West*, v. 2, pp. 141-77.

14. *Revue Thomiste* 4 (1896), pp. 413-41.

15. Anton E. van Hoff, O.S.B., "Die Innenseite des Modernismus," *Stimmen der Zeit* 113 (1989), pp. 667-76.

16. *Ibid.*

17. See Aubert, *L'Acte de Foi*, pp. 337-55.

18. Gilbert, "Die dritte Scholastik in Frankreich," in *Christliche Philosophie in katholischen Denken*, v. 2, pp. 423-25.

19. "Les Resources du Vouloir," *Revue Thomiste* 7 (1899), pp. 447-61.

20. "Les Exigences Objectives de l'Action," *Revue Thomiste* 6 (1898), pp. 125-38.

21. *Ibid.*

22. "L'Action: See "Ressources Subjectives," *Revue Thomiste* 7 (1899) pp. 23-39; "Les Ressources du Vouloir," *Revue Thomiste* 7 (1899), pp. 447-461; 377-99; "Ce qu'il y a du Vrai dans le Néo-Scotisme," *Revue Thomiste* 8 (1900) pp. 531-50; 648-65; and 9 (1901), pp. 407-43.

23. *Le Donné Révelé et la Théologie* (Paris: Gabala, 1910).

24. *Le Donné Révelé*, p. 13.

25. *Le Donné Révelé*, p. 10.

26. For an excellent exposition of Gardeil's philosophy of knowledge see Van Riet, *L'Épistémologie Thomiste*, pp. 244-62; 425-31.

27. See Aubert, *L'Acte de Foi*, pp. 395-450.

28. *La Crédibilité et l'Apologétique* (Paris: Gabala, 1908).

29. Aubert, *L'Acte de Foi*, pp. 396-400; 422-28.

30. *La Structure de l'Ame et l'Expérience Mystique*, 2 vols (Paris: Gabala, 1927). See Van Riet, *L'Épistémologie Thomiste*, pp. 425-31.

31. "L'Évolution de l'Intellectualisme Grec de Thalès a Aristote," *Revue Thomiste*, 7 (1913), pp. 5-23.

32. "La Révolution Cartésienne," *Revue de Sciences Philosophiques et Théologiques*, 4 (1910), pp. 678-93.

33. "Note sur la Théorie Thomiste de la Vérité," *Revue des Sciences Philosophiques et Théologiques*, 10 (1921), pp. 222-34.

34. "La Théorie Thomiste de l'Erreur," in *Mélanges Thomistes*, (Kain: Le Saulchoir, 1923), pp. 253-274, esp. pp. 268-69.

35. *Essai d'une Critique de la Connaissance*, (Paris: Vrin, 1932).

36. For a first rate account of Roland-Gosselin's epistemology see Van Riet, *L'Épistémologie Thomiste*, pp. 433-70.

37. Gilbert, "Die dritte Scholastik in Frankreich," in *Christliche Philosophie im katholischen Denken*, v. 2, pp. 426-29. For Garrigou-Lagrange's epistemology see Van Riet, *L'Épistémologie Thomiste*, pp. 338-49. For a brief English summary of his philosophy see Helen James John, *The Thomist Spectrum*, (New York: Fordham University Press, 1966), pp. 3-15.

38. Aubert, *L'Acte de Foi*, pp. 443-50.

39. *Le Sens Commun, la Philosophie de l'Etre et les Formules Dogmatiques*, (Paris: Beauchesne, 1909). Third edition (Paris: Nouvelle Librairie Nationale, 1922). Citations are from the third edition. For Le Roy's views on faith see Aubert, *L'Acte de Foi*, pp. 362-68.

40. *Le Sens Commun*, pp. 58-59.

41. *Dieu: son Existence et sa Nature* (Paris: Beauchesne, 1938). First edition was in 1915. E.T. *God: His Existence and His Nature*, 2 vols. (St. Louis: Herder, 1934).

42. *God: His Existence and his Nature*, v. I, pp. 110-11.

43. *Le Sens Commun*, pp. 58-59; 134-35.

44. *Reality: A Synthesis of Thomistic Thought*, St. Louis: Herder, 1950), pp. 31-57.

45. *Le Réalisme due Principe de Finalité*, (Paris: Desclée de Brouwer, 1932), p. 257.

46. *God: His Existence and His Nature*, v. I, pp. 139-205.

47. *God: His Existence and His Nature*, v. I, pp. 242-379.

48. The second volume of God: *His Existence and His Nature* is devoted to the divine attributes.

49. Garrigou-Lagrange's theological system is presented in *Reality: A Synthesis of Thomistic Thought*.

50. *De Revelatione per Ecclesiam Catholicam Proposita: Prior Pars Apologeticae* (Rome: Ferrari, 1925).

51. *The Three Ways of the Spiritual Life*, (London: Burns, Oates and Washbourne, 1938). See also *Reality: A Synthesis of Thomistic Thought*, p. 318 ff.

52. *Christian Perfection and Contemplation According to St. Thomas and St. John of the Cross* (St. Louis: Herder, 1937).

Chapter Four
The Thomism of Jacques Maritain

Maritain began his work before the First World War. He acquired his world wide reputation between the two wars and continued to write in defense of his approach to philosophy after Vatican II. Thus his career as a writer and lecturer extended through the growth and flowering of Neo-Thomism in the first half of the twentieth century until after its decline after the Second Vatican Council. In many respects he was the movement's best known representative and, in both Europe and American, he was a major force in Catholic thought for more than half a century. In addition to *The Degrees of Knowledge, Science and Wisdom, Quatre Essais sur l'Esprit dans sa Condition Charnelle* several other expositions of his epistemology and metaphysics were very well known.[1] Among them were *Introduction to Logic, A Preface to Metaphysics, Introduction to Philosophy, Philosophy of Nature, The Range of Reason,* and *Existence and the Existent.*[2] His opposition to Post-Cartesian philosophy, "separated" by its method from the Catholic faith, made itself plain in a number of his early works, such as *Bergsonian Philosophy and Thomism, Three Reformers,* and *The Dream of Descartes.*[3] Later in his career his philosophical reflection extended into the areas of aesthetics, politics, culture, and education. *Art and Scholasticism* and *Creative Intuition in Art and Poetry* continue to be read today, and in 1973 a new edition of *Integral Humanism* was brought out.[4] Between the two wars, and especially after the Second World War, Maritain's political philosophy served as an inspiration to the Christian Democratic movements in Europe and Latin America. *The Things That Are Not Caesar's, Freedom in the Modern World, Man and the State, The Person and the Com-*

mon Good and Maritain's *Moral Philosophy* were frequently cited titles in the 50s and 60s. After Vatican II, *The Peasant of the Garonne*, in which Maritain adopted a polemic attitude toward a number of the Post-Conciliar developments in Catholic thought, provoked lively critical reaction.[5]

Unlike other distinguished laymen among the Neo-Thomists, like Maurice De Wulf or Étienne Gilson, Maritain had no trace of Catholicism in his intellectual background. Both he and his wife, Raïssa, were agnostics, and neither of their families was in any way religious. Both Maritains had a remarkable grasp of the secular culture of their age. Jacques was a trained biologist and a gifted speculative philosopher endowed with more than ordinary literary talent. Raïssa was a talented poet. For many years the Maritain home became a center in which musicians, authors, and artists congregated.

Bergsonianism and Thomism.

Like many young people of their generation Jacques and Raïssa Maritain had found in the philosophy of Bergson the answer to their intellectual and spiritual needs. Bergson's metaphysics of liberty, process, and novelty gave the meaning to their lives which the determinism of the empiricist and Kantian philosophy taught in the French universities had failed to provide.[6] Jacques Maritain became an ardent Bergsonian and set about preparing himself for a career as a professor of philosophy.

However the Maritains's conversion to Catholicism soon upset the young philosopher's plans. Unlike Étienne Gilson, who never saw any conflict between his faith and a career in the state university system, Maritain felt that, in the anti-Catholic climate of the French Republic, a serious Catholic could have no hope for a university career. Consequently he gave up his plans to prepare himself for one.

Very soon after that initial sacrifice, the Church's condemnation of Modernism seemed to demand another. The Bergsonian philosophy, of whose truth Maritain was intellectually convinced, conceded no more than a purely practi-

cal value to the abstract concept. There was no place in it
either for the stable speculative conceptual knowledge which
the Church employed to justify her abiding dogmatic statements, nor was there any place in it for the analogy of being
which the Church's theologians used to justify our human
knowledge of the infinite transcendent God. Maritain felt
unable to defend either the scholastic epistemology of the
concept or the scholastic metaphysics of being and its analogy. Yet apparently the Church, in whose infallible teaching
he had come to believe, required him to adhere to their validity. In that case an insoluble conflict had arisen between
his two most profound intellectual convictions, the truth of his
Bergsonian philosophy and the truth of his Catholic faith. He
would have to choose one or the other. As a Catholic Maritain
decided to choose his faith, and, if he could not philosophize in
harmony with it, he would give up philosophy.

He was saved from that painful choice by his wife's Dominican spiritual director, Humbert Clerissac.[7] Once Clerissac had introduced him to St. Thomas, Maritain was convinced that in the Angelic Doctor, as the French Dominicans understood him, the epistemology and metaphysics
could be found which could do full justice to what was best
in Bergsonianism and at the same time correct what was deficient in it. Maritain was no longer forced to choose between Bergson and the Catholic faith, for, once Bergson's
philosophy had been corrected by St. Thomas, Bergsonianism and Catholicism became compatible.[8]

Bergson's influence can be discerned in the important
role assigned to intellectual intuition in Maritain's own philosophy. Nonetheless, Maritain's conversion to St. Thomas
was a thorough one, and the epistemology and metaphysics
which he used brilliantly in *The Degrees of Knowledge* had been
inspired by Thomas's great Dominican Commentators. Both
Jacques and Raïssa Maritain were ardent Catholics whose
intellectual lives were nourished by contemplative prayer.
Like Garrigou-Lagrange and the Carmelite Thomists of
Salamanca, Maritain was a disciple of St. John of the Cross,
and, although he always claimed to be no more than a phi-

losopher, he had a solid grasp of traditional Dominican spirituality and of the Thomistic theology associated with it.
Garrigou-Lagrange was one of his favorite theologians,[9] and,
despite Maritain's philosophical originality and the unique rich-
ness of his personal religious and aesthetic experience, there
were similarities between the integration of knowledge which
Garrigou-Lagrange had advocated and the integration which
Maritain himself worked out in *The Degrees of Knowledge.*

Direct Realism and the "Eidetic Intuition of Being."

One of these similarities was Maritain's direct realism
grounded upon his "eidetic intuition" of being.[10] Like the
Dominican Neo-Thomists, Maritain would have nothing to
do with a starting point for philosophy in consciousness.[11]
He stood with Étienne Gilson against the use of Kant's Transcendental Method which the Maréchalian Thomists were
willing to employ. Again, like Garrigou-Lagrange, he refused
to make philosophy of knowledge, as Descartes had made
it, the gateway to philosophical reflection. Epistemology belonged where Aristotle had put it, in the metaphysics which
followed his realistic philosophy of nature.[12]

As Garrigou-Lagrange had done, Maritain held that the
foundation of a realistic philosophy was the mind's immediate grasp of being through an "eidetic intuition." This intuition could not be simply, as Bergson had claimed, the mind's
immediate grasp of finite spirit's endless motion. For the
mind's awareness of its own activity came only through its
reflection on the prior affirmation of an extramental object
in the judgment. Every judgment, however, stood under the
necessary and universal intelligibility of the principle of identity; and that stable and all-embracing intelligibility transcended the mobility of finite mind and matter.[13] Thus the
intelligibility under which every judgment stood could manifest itself only through the stable *eidos* or intentional form of
being's abstract concept.[14] And, in that case, the metaphysics grounded upon the mind's immediate intuition of reality
could not be the process metaphysics of Bergson. It could
only be St. Thomas's metaphysics of act and potency in

which, contrary to Bergson's claim, motion must be understood in terms of being.[15]

It is not surprising, then, that in Maritain's *The Degrees of Knowledge* being is defined as essence, as the Dominican Neo-Thomists had defined it. For it is essence rather than existence which is grasped in the concept. In his later philosophy, however, and especially in *Existence and the Existent*, Maritain expanded and revised his epistemology of the "eidetic intuition." Two considerations moved him to do so: historical research into St. Thomas's text and his own appreciation of the role of immediate intellectual intuition in the grasp of reality.

Research into St. Thomas's account of the distinction of the sciences in *In Boethium de Trinitate*, subsequent to the publication of *The Degrees of Knowledge*, revealed that, contrary to the teaching of his Second Scholasticism Commentators, St. Thomas had not taught that the being on which metaphysics was grounded was known through the abstraction of its concept. On the contrary, the Angelic Doctor believed that the being of metaphysics was known through a *separation*, or negative judgment, through which the unique intelligibility of the act of existence was distinguished from any type of essential or formal intelligibility. Étienne Gilson then had strong support for his claim that Cajetan's theory of the three degrees of conceptual abstraction, around which Maritain had built *The Degrees of Knowledge*, did not represent the teaching of St. Thomas. For St. Thomas the intelligibility of being was not the intelligibility of *essence*, actual or possible. Rather it was the *intelligibility of existence*, grasped in the mind's affirmation that a sensible object *is*. The mind's prior grasp of *existence* made its subsequent negative judgment distinguishing existence from essence possible.

In *Existence and the Existent* Maritain endeavored to reconcile the epistemology of *The Degrees of Knowledge* with the results of later historical research. In the mind's first affirmation of an extramental object, he claimed, the human intellect *simultaneously* formed its first idea and uttered its first judgment of existence. Thus its first idea of being arose in the heart of a judgment of existence. Later on the metaphysician could clarify the content of this idea in the eidetic intuition associated with the third degree of abstraction. Then the intelligibility of being was explicitly disengaged from the intelligibility of mathematical or physical being.[16] Again in *A Preface to Metaphysics* Maritain linked the mind's grasp of the intelligibility of concrete existence to a pre-conceptual intuition. That intuition, he added, was a concrete, highly personal experience, akin to an intellectual shock or to a grace of the natural order. No conceptual knowledge could substitute for it, and without it even philosophers as great as Kant could not hope to be metaphysicians.[17]

Maritain's further development of the theory of the "eidetic intuition of being" carried it far beyond the sketchy outline provided by Garrigou-Lagrange. Despite that, however, questions can still be raised about its clarity and its overall coherence. Can a grasp of essence reached through the third degree of conceptual abstraction fit easily together with a grasp of concrete existence through the mind's affirmation that a sensible object *is*? How is the intellectual shock, or the natural grace, of the metaphysician's intuition of being related to the intuition of begin which every mind must have in order to justify Maritain's direct realism?

The Cognitional Sign.

Roland-Gossselin, as we have seen, turned to St. Thomas's metaphysics of the *species* or intentional form to justify the Thomistic realism of his own epistemology. As an intentional form, he explained, the *species* was relative by its very nature. It was a *medium quo*, a formal or cognitional sign, whose function was to refer the mind directly to the extramental object intentionally present in it. Maritain came upon the same metaphysics of the *species* or cognitional sign in the *Logic* of the great Second Scholasticism Thomist, John of St. Thomas.[18] But the use which he made of it was much more extensive. For Roland-Gosselin the cognitional sign had been the key to a Thomistic realism. For Maritain it became the key to his integration of knowledge.

Besides the concept there were many other cognitional signs. Each performed its own proper function by making extramental reality present to the mind in a specifically different way. The immediate act of awareness through which the human knower grasped his own reality made him aware of the world of extramental objects intentionally identified with his cognitive faculties through the multitude of diverse formal signs.

Maritain distinguished very carefully between the knower's concomitant self-awareness and the diverse types of objective knowledge acquired through the multitude of cognitional signs. This enabled him to apply his metaphysics of the formal sign to the religious, aesthetic, moral, and scientific realms of experience. Acts of sense knowledge, including the phantasm of the imagination, were distinct types of cognitional sign. Affective acts and habits, whether of natural love or supernatural charity, were cognitional signs of a very different sort, for connaturality, the love which made the lover like the object of his love, became a medium of knowledge through which the object of his connatural affection could be *known* in a distinctive way.[19]

In every cognitional sign an extramental object was intentionally identified with the knowing subject. The concept alone however enabled the knower to distinguish clearly between his own reality as a subject and the reality of the object present to him in the formal sign. Acts of sensation and affective states and habits, even spiritual acts and habits elevated to the supernatural order, did not. Therefore sensation and affectivity were confined to the level of experience on which subject and object could not be clearly distinguished from each other. The concept alone raised the knower to the level of objective knowledge on which subject and object were clearly distinguished from each other in the judgment.[20]

Maritain exploited the distinction between experiential and conceptual knowledge brilliantly in his speculative integration of human knowledge. He depended on it to reconcile John of the Cross's mystical theology with the scientific theology of the Angelic Doctor in *The Degrees of Knowledge*.[21]

The Christian mystic enjoyed an experiential knowledge of
the Triune God, intentionally united to his soul through the
supernatural habit of charity. Experiential knowledge of God
through the cognitional sign of charity could not distinguish
between the reality of God and the reality of the human
knower. The judgment through which the theologian expressed his scientific knowledge of the revealing God made
this distinction clear. It should cause no surprise, then, that
the language in which John of the Cross described his experiential knowledge of God differed markedly from the metaphysical language of St. Thomas's scientific theology. The
God experienced in mystical encounter was the same God
of whom the theologian spoke in the concepts of scientific
discourse. The diversity of the two saints' language corre-
sponded to the diversity of signs through which the same
God was known.

Maritain also employed the distinction between experiential and scientific knowledge in his defense of natural mysticism in *Quatre Essais sur l'Esprit dans sa Condition Charnelle.*[22]
The Indian ascetic who had purified his mind of its images
and concepts through the discipline of yoga could acquire
experiential knowledge of his own substantial act of existence in the experience of the void. Since God was present in
the mystic's act of existence through His divine activity of
conservation, immediate contact with the mystic's act of created existence could lead to an encounter with the Absolute
on the level of nature. The experience would be a mystical
experience because, on the level of experience, the act of
existence could not be distinguished from the Absolute immediately present in it. Nevertheless, the experience did not
transcend the level of nature because the medium of knowledge, the cognitional sign, was the mystic's own act of existence
and not the supernatural habit of charity as it was in the Christian mystic's immediate experience of the Triune God.

Maritain employed the distinction once again to discrimi-
nate between existential and objective knowledge of the self
in *Existence and the Existent.*[23] He drew on it with great success to distinguish between the artist's experiential knowl-

edge of reality through the cognitional sign of the intellectualized phantasm and scientific conceptual knowledge in *Art
and Scholasticism* and *Creative Intuition in Art and Poetry*.[24] The
soul's experience of itself and God was not the objective
knowledge of scientific theology. Aesthetic experience could
not be equated with philosophy. The intrinsic aim of these
diverse forms of knowledge was not, and could not be, the
same. To make mysticism a substitute for theology or to make
art a substitute for philosophical self-knowledge was a fa-
tally destructive error. A proper appreciation of the nature
of each cognitional sign and a clear discrimination of each
sign's proper function were required for the successful integration of human knowledge.

The Distinction and Unification of the Sciences.

Cajetan's epistemology of the three degrees of abstraction and Aristotle's account of the distinction of the sciences
gave Maritain the key to his integration of speculative knowledge. For Aristotle, the intelligibility of a sensible singular
was due to its form; matter, the principle of individuality had
no intrinsic intelligibility. Therefore the abstraction of a universal intentional form from a sensible singular could be compared to the abstraction of an intelligible form from matter.
Aristotle had grouped his speculative sciences in a hierarchy of three ascending genera, physics, mathematics, and
metaphysics, and Cajetan accounted for this hierarchy
through the successive stages in the abstraction of an intelligible form from matter. Thus, for Cajetan, Aristotle's distinction of the sciences was explained through the three degrees of formal abstraction. In the first degree of abstraction
the mind abstracted an intelligible form from sensible matter. This was the level of mobile being, the world of Aristotelian physics or philosophy of nature. In the second degree of
abstraction, the mind abstracted from the "sensible matter"
of mobile being and focussed its attention on the "intelligible
matter" of discrete and continuous quantity. This was the
level of Aristotelian mathematics. On the third degree of
abstraction, the mind abstracted from all matter. This was
the level of metaphysics, the science of being itself.[25]

The three distinct genera, based on the three degrees of
conceptual abstraction, freed philosophy from the univocal
notion of science inherited from Descartes and from the univocal notion of scientific method which Descartes had in-
flicted on it. In Aristotle's hierarchy of the sciences, each
genus had its own unique formal intelligibility and its own
distinctive method. Science, like the being on which it was
grounded, was seen to be an analogous notion. Philosophical science — which began on the level of physics or philosophy of nature — could be clearly distinguished from the modern empirical sciences whose legitimate field of investiga-
tion was restricted to the phenomenal world.[26]

Metaphysics then could resume its legitimate work as
an Aristotelian "wisdom,"[27] philosophy's "ruling science,"
whose function it was to determine the validity of its own
principles through its critical reflection on their foundations
and then to assign to the other sciences their proper role in
the acquisition and control of human knowledge.[28] In *The
Degrees of Knowledge* then, as we can see, Maritain was consciously taking up again the task assigned to the metaphysician by the Dominican Thomists of the Second Scholasticism. Like epistemology, the reflective integration of knowledge belonged to metaphysics.

Theology too was an Aristotelian science, made possible
through man's participation in the divine self-knowledge
manifested in revelation and communicated to the soul
through the infused supernatural habit of faith.[29] In theology therefore God was known in His own being and not
simply through philosophical reflection on the created ef-
fects of His causality. Furthermore, the first principles
grasped through the supernatural light of faith gave firmer
certitude to its conclusions than any naturally known first
principles could give them. Theology then, given the superior nature of its knowledge, was the highest "ruling science"
or "wisdom."[30] Above it was only the highest of all wisdoms
attainable in this life, the wisdom of the great mystics like
St. John of the Cross. This higher, mystical wisdom, however, could never be a science. For the cognitional sign

through which its knowledge of God was reached was not the cognitional sign of the concept required for objective knowledge. Rather it was the cognitional sign of the infused habit of charity, and the knowledge of God communicated by it was the interior "ineffable knowledge" of the God so intimately present to the soul that the distinction between subject and object did not appear.[31]

The Integration of Practical Knowledge.

Maritain's "eidetic intuition" of being and the analogy of being and of the sciences, built upon the three degrees of formal abstraction which Maritain had taken over from Cajetan's epistemology, made possible the integration of speculative knowledge which he worked out in *The Degrees of Knowledge*. Despite the brilliance of that integration, Maritain's more lasting contribution to philosophy was made through his more original work in ethics, politics and aesthetics. As we have seen, Post-Cartesian philosophy had neglected the significant distinction between the knower's immediate grasp of his own acts of knowing and desiring and the objective knowledge of his own and of extramental reality acquired through the cognitional sign of the concept. It had also downplayed another important distinction which the Neo-Thomists had returned to its proper place of prominence in the philosophy of knowledge. This was Aristotle's classic distinction between the theoretical and practical use of the intellect.

Maritain made good use of that distinction in *Art and Scholasticism*. Man is more than a scientific knower whose speculative judgments are conformed to existing essences through concepts abstracted from sense experience. Man is also a "doer" and a "maker" whose practical intellect participates in God's creative knowledge. Through his moral action, the human agent brings his nature to the fullness of its specific perfection. He makes himself a "good man." Through his productive action, man, "the maker," *homo faber*, imposes an intelligible form on matter through the activity of his mind and hand. He "makes" a "good work." This is true whether the works produced serve the practical needs of an "artisan" who makes them or whether the works serve as the symbolic "word" through which the creative artist expresses his response to the beauty of the corporeal world intentionally present within him.[32] Art is not speculative knowledge because the cognitional sign through which the creative artist "speaks his word" is not the objective cognitional sign of the concept. On the contrary, it is the cognitional sign of the artistic symbol, the work of art, in which subject and object are not clearly distinguished.

The norm which governs truth in the practical use of the intellect cannot be the norm which governs truth in its speculative use. For neither the perfection of the moral agent nor the "work" to be produced by the artist are as yet existing essences. They are no more than ideal ends toward which the process of "making" or "doing" are directed by the practical knowledge of the human agent.[33] Conformity of the mind to its object then cannot be viewed, as it is in speculative knowledge, as the conformity of a Platonic "image" to an existing essence as its "exemplar." On the contrary, practical knowledge of the "deed to be done" or of the "work to be made" serves as a creative Platonic exemplar to which the projected "deed" or "work" must conform itself as a Platonic "image" or "likeness."

Thus the truth of the practical intellect is determined by the "straight appetite," the tendency which it directs toward its proper goal, the moral "deed" or the artistic "work."

The production of a morally good person is not the same goal as the production of a good work of art. This diversity of goals, Maritain, observed is the basis of the celebrated distinction between "prudence" and "art" as virtues of the practical intellect. Christians would be well advised to pay proper attention to that distinction. It could protect them against the error into which they often fall, the confusion of aesthetic with moral values. A work can be good art without being morally edifying and a work can be morally edifying without being good art.[35]

The distinction between the practical and speculative use of the intellect also served Maritain well in his account of moral knowledge. Ethics was a practical science whose rigorously formulated general principles directed human action toward its natural end, the development of a good human person.[36] Those principles, however, had been acquired through generalizations from the singular prudential judgments made by the morally good agents who had been rendered "connatural," or morally sensitive to the values at stake through their habitual good behavior. The deductions from general principles to individual applications needed to guide concrete action required similar prudential judgments about singular actions; and these in turn would only be made well habitually by agents whose previous conduct had rendered them sensitive to the values at stake. As they did in the ethics of Aristotle and St. Thomas, prudence and connaturality went together in Maritain's moral philosophy. His ethics could never be an impersonal science on the Post-Cartesian model—as was the ethics of John Locke (1632-1704)—modelled on the sciences of the speculative intellect.

Further, since knowledge of man's actual end was required for the practical intellect to be able to direct his activity toward it, Maritain concluded that, although the practical science of ethics must retain its philosophical character, it could not function effectively unless it were subordinated to moral theology. In the real order man's concrete end was the Beatific Vision (the vision of God) and elevation of the soul by grace was required to reach it. Man's concrete nature had been so wounded by Original Sin that, without the aid of grace, habitually good action was no longer within his power.[37] Left to its own resources, moral philosophy could acquire no knowledge of these truths. Without that knowledge however, man's practical intellect could not conform itself to the "straight appetite" which tended toward man's real end. For the truth of the practical intellect then, moral philosophy had to take over these truths from the he higher science of moral theology.[38]

Maritain's Political Philosophy.

Before the First World War many French Neo-Thomists were royalist in their politics and considered the anticlerical French republic an illegitimate form of government. As a young man Maritain had been a republican with socialist sympathies and, after his conversion, he did not concern himself with polities. After the First World war, however, Pius XI condemned the *Action Française*, the reactionary authoritarian movement led by Charles Maurras, who was not himself a Christian. Maritain then broke with the right wing Thomists by supporting the Pope in *The Things That Are Not Caesar's.*[39] His break with them marked the beginning of his career as a Thomistic defender of representative democracy.

For Maritain, as it had been for St. Thomas, politics was part of a natural law ethics. Legitimate moral authority in civil society was given by God to the ruler charged with the duty of directing a society toward its natural end, the common good. In the Second Scholasticism, theologians, such as Francis Suarez and Robert Bellarmine (1542-1621), had argued that the holder of God-given authority was designated by the members of a given civil society, and that its government could take many legitimate forms. Their argument gave strong support to the opponents of royal absolutism in France and England, but, of itself, it did not require that the consent of the people should express itself through the representative form of government found in the parliamentary democracies to which the right-wing Catholics were opposed.

Maritain was able to do so, however, through his extension of St. Thomas's philosophy of person and community. As a form received in matter, man was an individual, shut off from every other subsistent being. Yet, as a created participant in God's infinite existence, he was also an agent who shared in existence's "expansive generosity."[40] More than that, he was a free and spiritual agent. Through the activity of his speculative and practical intellect and through the free choices of his will, he was called to speak his unique and irreplaceable word of response to the world and to its Creator.[41] Man was an individual human nature but he was also a person.

As a human nature, man was a member of society obliged to cooperate in achieving the common good under the direction of legitimate authority. But he was also a free person called to tend directly toward God as his immediate end. His duty to tend toward God directly gave him his fundamental rights as a human person which could never be disregarded in the interest of society's common good.[42] Thus, neither the radical individualism of Locke's liberalism, nor the collectivism of Marxian socialism were compatible with sound social ethics.

The authoritarian forms of government, which some European Catholics favored, Maritain argued, were no longer legitimate forms of government in modern western society. Growth in intellectual maturity and in the capacity to exercise his personal freedom was an exigency of man's human nature. Therefore, society was obliged to foster such development rather than impede it. Consequently the state should not reserve to itself the direction of human activity which psychologically mature people and their societies could freely assume themselves. Authoritarian forms of government, which were tolerable before Western man achieved his present state of cultural and personal development, were no longer acceptable today. Society must recognize that modern man is a social and cultural adult. Contemporary man must recognize society's legitimate power to direct his action toward the common good. Nevertheless his claim to be given a share in society's decisions was justified.[43] In developed Western society, democratic self government was not required by the natural law for the legitimate exercise of authority. Maritain's defense of democracy, express in *The Things That Are Not Caesar's, Freedom and The Modern World*, and *Man and the State*, helped to inspire the Christian Democratic movements which flourished in Europe and North America after the Second World War.

Creative Intuition.

Maritain's first in-depth reflection on St. Thomas's philosophy of art was found in his *Art and Scholasticism*, but his own most original contribution to Thomistic aesthetics was made in *Creative Intuition in Art and Poetry*. In this later work he drew on his philosophy of intuition and of the cognitional sign to examine the nature of aesthetic knowledge. Intellectual emotion, he explained, like other affective states, can transform itself into a cognitional sign.[45] Below the level of clearly differentiated conscious knowledge, we find the vaguer, undifferentiated level of "preconscious" images and feelings. These images and feelings are still conscious, and they are penetrated by the spiritual dynamism and the personal freedom of the human knower.[46] On this lower level of knowledge, the clear distinction between subject and object, achieved through the cognitional sign of the concept, does not yet exist. This means that the artist's "pre-conceptual awareness" of the concrete world, intentionally identified with his own being through his intellectualized emotion, is an intuition.[47]

It is, however, an intuition of a special sort, a "creative intuition." For the artist, in his personal response to the beauty manifested in the world, does not express himself through the "word" of a conceptual judgment. He speaks his "word" by imposing an intelligible form on matter through the production of a symbol, his work of art.[48] As a producer, the artist participates in God's creative knowledge. He does so through his "creative intuition," the intellectualized emotion through which the concrete world unites itself to him in the intentional order.[49]

Like God then, the artist produces his work by knowing himself, and his work of art is a "generous outpouring" of his own existence. Self-expression though it may be, it is not self-enclosed or egotistical.[50] As a response to beauty, loved through its manifestation in the world, the production of an artwork is, in its own way, a tendency to the infinite. No concrete art work however can be an adequate expression of the infinite; and so infinite beauty can only be the "end

beyond the end" toward which the process of artistic production is immediately directed.[51] Like every "making," the
production of an artwork must be guided by the virtue of
art. For every good artist must have a firm mastery of his
technique. But the artist's "creative intuition," the "seed"
within him from which the external artwork "flowers," is
quite different from art. The artist's "inspiration," the unique
intuition of beauty and the unique response to it in intellectualized sense which makes the great artist, should not be
reduced to mere technical ability.

Integral Humanism.

Among the major achievements of Maritain's philosophy had been its distinction and integration of the various
types and levels of human knowledge. The philosophy of
the Angelic Doctor, extended and applied through his own
initiative, was the instrument which had enabled him to do
that. As a philosophy, Maritain believed, St., Thomas's philosophy was a true philosophy in its nature, since it was independent of Christian revelation in its objects, principles,
and methods. Nevertheless, it was a Christian philosophy in
its state. For it was carried on by a Christian mind, elevated
by grace and preserved by its knowledge of revelation from
serious philosophical errors.[52]

As a matter of principle, Post-Cartesian philosophy had
separated itself from revelation. It had also abandoned the
Aristotelian philosophy of knowledge, man, and being which
St. Thomas had used to structure his own philosophy and
theology. Therefore, both in its state and in its nature, Post-
Cartesian philosophy was deficient. No wonder then that it
had shown itself unable to integrate speculative and practical knowledge, to distinguish between creative artistic knowledge and speculative philosophy, or to relate the mystic's
experience of God to sound theology.

Yet return to an undeveloped mediaeval philosophy was
not sufficient to integrate contemporary culture. The modern mind was no longer the mediaeval mind which had little
or no acquaintance with the multiplicity of cognitional signs

through which modern man thematizes his knowledge of himself and of his world in art, science, and history.[53] Modern culture has ceased to be the naive and relatively simple culture of the Middle ages. The created world has become aware of its relative autonomy and a multitude of modern disciplines have distinguished themselves from philosophy and theology. Scientific experience reached the stage of self-awareness in the seventeenth and eighteenth centuries; Christian mysticism had already reached that stage in the time of St. Theresa and of St. John of the Cross; aesthetical and historical experience reached it in the nineteenth century.

Maritain welcomed these developments as progressive stages in human growth. His *Integral Humanism* might make interesting reading for the critics of Neo-Thomism who assume that Thomists are unable to respond with welcome to modern culture. Far from being in love with the Middle Ages, Maritain was a modern man well acquainted with the literature, music, art, and science of his own age. Thomism did not appeal to him because it was mediaeval. He was drawn to it in the belief that, intelligently extended and applied, it could become, in capable hands, the philosophy which the modern world needed to integrate twentieth century experience; and, in his own effort to do so, Maritain made a good case in favor of his claim.

Notes

1. *The Degrees of Knowledge* (New York: Scribner's, 1959). *Science and Wisdom* (New York: Scribner's, 1940). *Quatre Essais sur l'Esprit dans sa Condition Charnelle* (Paris: Desclée de Brouwer, 1939).

2. *An Introduction to Logic* (New York: Sheed & Ward, 1937). *A Preface to Metaphysics Seven Lessons on Being* (New York: Sheed & Ward, 1948). *Philosophy of Nature* (New York: Philosophical Library, 1951). *The Range of Reason* (New York: Scribner's, 1952). *Existence and the Existent* (New York: Pantheon, 1948).

3. *Bergsonian Philosophy and Thomism* (New York: Philosophical Library, 1955). *Three Reformers: Luther, Descartes, Rousseau* (New York: Philosophical Library, 1944). *The Dream of Descartes, Together with Some Other Essays* (New York: Philosophical Library, 1944).

4. *Art and Scholasticism* (New York: Scribner's, 1962). *Creative Intuition in Art and Poetry* (New York: Pantheon, 1953; repr. New York: Meridian, 1955). *Integral Humanism: Temporal and Spiritual Problems of a New Christendom* (Notre Dame: University of Notre Dame Press, 1973).

5. *The Things That Are Not Caesar's* (New York: Scribner's 1931). *Freedom in the Modern World* (New York: Scribner's, 1936). *Man and the State* (Chicago: The University of Chicago Press, 1951). *The Person and the Common Good* (Notre Dame: University of Notre Dame Press, 1973). *Moral Philosophy: An Historical and Critical Survey of the Great Systems* (New York: Scribner's, 1964). *The Peasant of the Garonne: An Old Layman Questions Himself about the Present Time* (New York: Holt, Rinehart and Winston, 1968).

6. Julie Kernan, *Our Friend, Jacques Maritain* (Garden City: Doubleday, 1975), pp. 15-25.

7. Kernan, *Our Friend, Jacques Maritain,* pp. 40-42.

8. *Bergsonian Philosophy and Thomism,* pp. 5-60, esp. pp. 18-20. See also pp. 289-94.

9. Kernan, *Our Friend, Jacques Maritain,* pp. 59 and 77. For Maritain's theological orientation see Charles Journet, "Jacques Maritain: Theologian," *The New Scholasticism* 46 (1972), pp. 32-50.

10. *Bergsonian Philosophy and Thomism,* pp. 35, 308-09, *A Preface to Metaphysics,* pp. 43-51, *Existence and the Existent,* pp. 19-22.

11. *The Degree of Knowledge,* pp. 71-74, 107-08, 128-29, 153-54. For a clear and comprehensive account of Maritain's epistemology see Van Riet, *L'Épistémologie Thomiste,* pp. 349-75.

12. *The Degrees of Knowledge,* pp. 78-80.

13. *A Preface to Metaphysics,* pp. 57-58.

14. *The Degrees of Knowledge*, pp. 95-99, 121-23; *A Preface to Metaphysics*, pp. 43-45.

15. *Bergsonian Philosophy and Thomism*, pp. 114-16; *A Preface to Metaphysics*, pp. 74-75.

16. *Existence and the Existent*, pp. 22-35.

17. *A Preface to Metaphysics*, pp. 45-49. See also *The Degrees of Knowledge*, pp. 278-80.

18. *Science and Wisdom*, pp. 103-04.

19. *Science and Wisdom*, pp. 112-14.

20. *Ibid.*, pp. 113-14.

21. *The Degrees of Knowledge*, pp. 310-51.

22. *Quatre Essais sur l'Esprit dans sa Condition Charnelle*, pp. 131-77. For an English translation, see Jacques Maritain, *Challenges and Renewals: Selected Readings*, ed. Joseph W. Evans and Leo Ward (Notre Dame: University of Notre Dame Press, 1966), pp. 76-106.

23. *Existence and the Existent*, pp. 76-84. See also Henry Bars, "Sujet et Subjectivité selon Jacques Maritain," *Les Études Philosophiques*, (1975), pp. 31-46.

24 *Art and Scholasticism*, pp. 5-32, *Creative Intuition in Art and Poetry*, pp. 75-108.

25. *The Degrees of Knowledge*, pp. 38-40, 53-54, 136-37, 176-77, 210-11. See also *Science and Wisdom*, pp. 42-44, 57-64, and *A Preface to Metaphysics*, pp. 43-45, 58-59.

26. *The Degrees of Knowledge*, pp. 138-39, 194-95. See Jean-Louis Allard, "Maritain's Epistemology of Modern Science: A Summary Presentation," in *Jacques Maritain's The Degrees of Knowledge: A Conference Seminar*, ed. Robert Henle, S.J., Marion Cordes and Jeanne Vatterott (Saint Louis: The American Maritain Association, 1981), pp. 144-73.

27. *Science and Wisdom*, pp. 23-24; *The Degrees of Knowledge*, pp. 247-48.

28. *The Degrees of Knowledge*, pp. 40-41, 79-80, 247-48.

29. *The Degrees of Knowledge*, pp. 251-52.

30. *Science and Wisdom*, pp. 194-95.

31. *The Degrees of Knowledge*, pp. 257-65.

32. *Art and Scholasticism*, pp. 7-32. See also *Creative Intuition in Art and Poetry*, pp. 31-41.

33. *Art and Scholasticism*, pp. 14-16. *Creative Intuition in Art and Poetry*, pp. 40-45.

34. *Art and Scholasticism*, pp. 19-20.

35. *Art and Scholasticism*, pp. 36-38.

36. *Science and Wisdom*, pp. 113-14.

37. *Science and Wisdom*, pp. 145-54, 194-205, 210-20.

38. *Science and Wisdom*, pp. 161-67, 210-12.

39. Kernan, *Our Friend, Jacques Maritain*, pp. 70-84.

40. *Creative Intuition in Art and Poetry*, pp. 105-07.

41. Jacques Maritain, *Scholasticism and Politics* (New York: Macmillan, 1940), pp. 78-79.

42. *The Person and the Common Good*, pp. 31-46.

43. *Man and the State*, pp. 84-94, 126-29. See Also Gerald A. McCool, S.J., "Maritain's Defense of Democracy," *Thought* 54 (1979), pp. 132-42.

44. See Alceu Amoroso Lima, "The Influence of Maritain in Latin America," *The New Scholasticism* 46 (1972), pp. 70-85.

45. *Creative Intuition in Art and Poetry*, pp. 87-88.

46. *Ibid.*, pp. 66-67, 78-80.

47. *Ibid.*, pp. 80-90.

48. *Ibid.*, pp. 31-41, 72-74.

49. *Ibid.*, pp. 80-82, 100-01.

50. *Ibid.*, pp. 105-08.

51. *Ibid.*, pp. 128-35.

52. Jacques Maritain, *An Essay on Christian Philosophy* (New York: Philosophical Library, 1955), pp. 11-29.

53. *Integral Humanism*, pp. 9-15.

Chapter Five
Pierre Rousselot

The form of Neo-Thomism which was later called Transcendental Thomism traces its origin to two Jesuit Thomists, Pierre Rousselot (1878-1915) and Joseph Maréchal, who was a professional philosopher. Rousselot was a theologian whose primary concern was with the problems of faith and reason which faced the Church at the beginning of the twentieth century. Nevertheless he was a very philosophical theologian. In his opinion philosophy and theology were linked to each other "like matter and form to make a unitary whole."[1] If then his theology was to be an effective one, he believed, it must be structured by a coherent philosophy sufficiently inclusive and rigorous to deal with the problems of the present day.

Those problems were the same ones with which Ambroise Gardeil had to grapple before and during the Modernist crisis: the relation between natural reason, to which apologetics was directed, and the free and supernatural act of faith, the relation between historical religious experience and the Church's abiding dogmas, and the possibility of conceptual knowledge of God through the analogy of being. Bergsonian philosophy, the voluntarism of James's pragmatism and Blondel's philosophy of action — both known as "Neo-Scotism" among French Catholics — and the immanentism of Kantian idealism had focussed attention on these problems in the first decade of the century.

Rousselot shared Gardeil's conviction that the metaphysics of St. Thomas was the philosophy to which the Catholic theologian should turn to structure the theology which could deal with this set of problems. He did not, however, like Gardeil and his disciples, read St. Thomas in the light of the Second Scholasticism tradition of his own religious order.

On the contrary, he abandoned the Suarezianism, still popular at that time in the Society of Jesus, and took his philosophy directly from the text of the Angelic Doctor himself.

His study of St. Thomas moreover was not a purely historical one. Its aim was to identify the fundamental principles, the "architectonic theses," of St. Thomas's metaphysics and to show how their relation to one another made the Angelic Doctor's theology a powerful, comprehensive, and coherent synthesis.[2] St. Thomas's theology could then be seen as a distinctive living whole. Its "architectonic theses" could be distinguished from the outmoded nonessential doctrines contained in it. They could also be extended and refined to meet the needs of modern thought; and, if need be, the consequences flowing from them could be employed to correct some of the inconsistencies in Thomas's actual practice.

When this historical work had been done, Thomism, put to work by the practicing theologian, could undertake the "necessary absorptions" of modern thought without endangering its own integrity. Historical study was only one of the means required for Thomism's vital development. Critical absorption of modern thought must be the other.[3] From the beginning then the Thomism of Rousselot and Maréchal adopted a more receptive attitude toward Blondel's philosophy of action and Kantian idealism than did Thomism in the tradition of Gardeil and Maritain.

Rousselot's major historical studies, *L'Intellectualisme de Saint Thomas* and *Pour L'Histoire: du Problème de l'Amour au Moyen-Age*[4] were both completed before his ordination to the priesthood. They were respectively the major and minor thesis required for his doctorate at the Sorbonne. Rousselot defended his major thesis publicly in 1908 and began to teach theology in Paris the following year when he joined the faculty at the Institut Catholique. With a single year's exception he continued his courses in faith and charity there until he was called to military service at the outbreak of the First World War. His short and brilliant career ended ten months later when he was killed in action at the age of thirty-seven.

The Problem of Love.

With an eye on contemporary "Neo-Scotism," *Le Problème de l'Amour* opposed the intellectualism of St. Thomas to the voluntarism or the mediaeval Franciscan theologians. For St. Thomas the created intellect, and not the created will, was the highest among the spiritual faculties. For the Angelic Doctor, union with God in the Beatific Vision, the spiritual creature's highest act, did not consist essentially in an act of love, as it did for Scotus. It consisted rather in an act of the intellect.[5] The union of the spiritual creature with God in its act of love was subsequent to and dependent on its prior and essential union with God through an act of intellectual intuition.[6]

A number of important philosophical consequences followed from St. Thomas's metaphysics of the Beatific Vision. The spiritual creature's supreme fulfillment was reached in an act of intellectual intuition. Human souls and angels attained their beatitude through an immediate grasp of their own essence and of God intentionally united to it through the "light of glory."[7] But that intentional union presupposed a prior union in being between finite knower and infinite known. For their prior union in being was the condition of possibility for effecting the subsequent intentional union of knower and known in the act of knowledge. Furthermore, since the blessed creatures do not lose their own substantial identity in the Beatific Vision, the union in being between infinite known and finite knower cannot exceed the unity based on participation.[9] Nevertheless, although the intellect which reaches its fulfillment through intentional unity with God is finite in its participated being, it must be infinite in the range of its knowledge.[9] The finite intellect then is a power ordered to intentional union with God as its natural end. Thus, in St. Thomas's metaphysics of knowledge, as Rousselot explained more fully in *L'Intellectualisme de Saint Thomas*, the intelligence is essentially the sense of the real only because it is the sense of the divine.[10] St. Thomas's metaphysics of the Beatific Vision therefore provided Rousselot key to a proper Thomistic understanding of the nature and power of the intellect.

Joined to his Aristotelian metaphysics of the faculties, Rousselot continued, St. Thomas's Platonic participation metaphysics explains how the in-built self-love which moves a created Aristotelian nature to action can terminate in the will's selfless love of God for His own sake in the supernatural act of charity. Every member of an organic whole, outside of which the part cannot exist, naturally loves the good of the whole on which it depends as its "own good." That is why St. Thomas said that, in an act of self-protection, the hand will sacrifice its own good for the good of the body. Yet the union between God's infinite existence and the created participant in it is more intimate than the union between part and whole in an organic totality. For without the uninterrupted communication of the divine existence, the essence which participates in it would be literally nothing. Therefore, in loving God, the created participant in His existence is literally loving its "own good."[11] Thus, far from being opposed to the self-love of an Aristotelian nature, as the Franciscan theologians thought, the supernatural act of charity, in which God is loved for His own sake, brings the natural self-love of a spiritual nature to its fulfillment.[12]

In *Le Problème de l'Amour* therefore Rousselot worked out a Thomistic synthesis focussed on the act of intellectual intuition, the natural finality of the intellect and will, and a metaphysics of participation in which existence, unlimited in God, is limited in its participation by the created essence which receives it.[13]

The Intellectualism of St. Thomas.

St. Thomas's metaphysics of the Beatific Vision, Rousselot argued in *L'Intellectualisme de Saint Thomas*, could also provide the necessary corrective to the false understanding of intellectualism prevalent in nineteenth century French philosophy and exemplified in its rationalist systems, as, for example, in the system of Léon Brunschvicq (1869-1944). In the rationalist understanding of the term, intellectualism's ideal of knowledge was modelled on the abstract universal concept. The highest form of knowledge was considered to be the all-inclusive unity of a system of clear and distinct ideas linked to one another in the necessary enchainment of a rigorous, deductive logic. Since Descartes had shown that reason was the same in every mind, intellectual knowledge had to be understood in the purely univocal sense assigned to it in Post-Cartesian rationalism. Intellectualism would then designate the impersonal, abstractly conceptual ideal of knowledge against which both Bergson and Blondel had reacted in their defense of life, intuition, freedom, and action; and, as could be seen in the late nineteenth century scholastic manuals, even Neo-Thomism had not escaped its influence.

St. Thomas's intellectualism, however, was of a very different sort. For the Angelic Doctor the concept was the lowest kind of intellectual knowledge.[14] His norm of perfection in knowledge was not the *ratio* of the conceptualist systems: it was *intellectus*, the intuitive knowledge which God and the pure spirits enjoyed of their own essence.[15] For God and the angels knew His creatures by knowing the created participants in His existence as the concrete terms of the act of free creative love identified with His own being.[16] Angels knew other beings through the *species* or intentional forms produced in their essence by God's act of creation.[17]

In St. Thomas's participation metaphysics no substantial form could be individuated unless it was received in pure matter. Thus, since angels were pure substantial forms, each angel must be the only individual which could exist in its own species; and so, in knowing its own substantial form through an act of *intellectus*, each angel also knew an individual. It knew an individual as well when it knew the substantial form of another angel through the intentional *species* produced in its mind by God. Since God alone could act upon pure spirits, the angel's knowledge of material beings could not be due to abstraction of a universal form from a sensible species. It too required the production of an intentional form in the angel's intellect by God's creative action. United to their specific form through the intentional form produced in its mind by God, the angel knew every existing individual in a material species as a concrete instantiation virtually precontained in its specific form as its "quasi-exemplar." Thus, in both the divine and the angelic mind, *intellectus*, as St. Thomas's ideal of perfect knowledge, was always an intellectual intuition of a concrete singular.[18]

It was also highly personal knowledge. God was the loving free creator of the universe and the personal goal to which the whole universe returned through the knowledge and love of its spiritual creatures in the Beatific Vision. In St. Thomas's metaphysics, the pure forms were not impersonal ideas; they were the angels, free living beings. In its highest form then, knowledge of God and of other living spirits, *intellectus*, meant "sharing in the life of another person." The sympathetic love for another being which came from "connatural likeness" to it enabled *intellectus* to penetrate to the unique singularity of everything which it knew. This was true of God's loving creative knowledge of the individuals who became likenesses of His existence by participating in it. It was true as well of angelic knowledge. Since the angel's created essence had to be distinct from its existence, the angel had to pass from potency to act in order to perform its finite act of knowledge. In other words, it had to "express itself" by "speaking a word" in its act of *intellectus*. Prior reception of an object's intentional form, however, was required for a potential finite intellect to "express itself" in its "word" of knowing another. Reception of that form in the mind of a pure spirit led to the "connatural" likeness between knower and known which in turn provoked the conscious "loving sympathy" through which the angel's knowledge penetrated to the unique singularity of the other's being.[19] In St. Thomas's intellectualism then, as in Blondel's philosophy of action, life, love, and freedom entered into the highest form of knowledge.

Furthermore, *intellectus*, as the highest form of knowledge, could not be understood univocally. Since every angel differed specifically from all the others, angelic minds formed a hierarchy of specifically distinct intellects. The higher an angel stood on the scale of being, the closer its mind approached to the comprehensive unity of God's absolutely simple intellect, and the fewer were the intentional forms or *species* required for its comprehension of the universe. Concentration *in* ideas rather than multiplication *of* ideas was the mark of perfection in St. Thomas's metaphysics of knowledge.[20] Every angel was a monad (a self-contained individual) and every angelic mind, even the highest, synthesized the universe in a specifically different way and viewed the world from its own unique finite point of view.[21] Only when angels and blessed souls "shared the life of God" and were able to know the world through God's mind in the Beatific Vision could a single unified intellectual comprehension of the universe by achieved.[22] "Absolute Knowledge" for St. Thomas could not take the form of a system of logically linked ideas. It was achieved by *intellectus* in the loving personal union between God and finite free spirits in the Beatific Vision.

Man's abstract universal concepts were no more than a deficient substitute for the angel's intuitive knowledge of itself and others.[23] As a form received in matter, man could have no intuitive knowledge of any essence, even of his own. *Intellectus* in man could go no further than the conscious awareness which he possessed of his own cognitive and appetitive operations. The concepts which the discursive human *ratio* abstracted from sense experience, far from being intuitions of the real, were no more than constructs of man's active intellect. Human knowledge of immaterial realities, such as God, the angels, or the human soul, could be gained only indirectly, through a process of affirmation and negation, from sense experience. Therefore, an element of unreality affected all conceptual knowledge. Unable to grasp the intelligible singularity of any real being, the universal concept subsumed the members of each species under the abstract unity of a "common nature." The multiple discursive concepts of the unitary nature's abstract definition, however, could not correspond to the singular reality of any material being's unitary substantial form.[24] And so, since the universal concept was never able to grasp things as they really are, it was condemned to know them indirectly through

"what they were not." Conceptual knowledge, even of material substances, could be no more than analogous. As
Rousselot put it rather bluntly, there was a touch of nominalism in St. Thomas's intellectualism.[25]

The imperfection of conceptual knowledge made the
strict unity which Aristotle required for the middle term of
his scientific syllogism impossible.[26] Therefore, although St.
Thomas himself did not advert to the fact, the theory of
knowledge which was one of his most original contributions
to philosophy, could not be reconciled with the Aristotelian
conception of science on which he had structured his own
theology. The *organon of* Aristotelian science, built on the
abstract concept, was a substitute for the totalizing vision of
the world achieved in angelic intuition. It knew nothing of
the singular and, unlike the angelic intuition, which knew
every material being and its place in the successive order of
its species, Aristotelian science had no knowledge of human
history. That was why the discursive intellect was compelled
to call on aesthetic knowledge and historical science of contingent events as further substitutes for its missing intuition.[27]
In opposition to the Maritain of *The Degrees of Knowledge*,
Rousselot concluded that St. Thomas's use of Aristotelian
scientific method was one of the inconsistencies in the Angelic Doctor's actual practice which better acquaintance with
St. Thomas's original theory of knowledge would enable his
disciples to correct. Many decades later, Bernard Lonergan
would make the same point when he worked out his own
anti-Aristotelian method for theology on the basis of St.
Thomas's philosophical study of *intellectus*, or, as Lonergan
called it, the act of insight.

Rousselot's Later Philosophical Articles.

Rousselot turned his attention to the judgment in the set
of articles which he published in 1910 as the philosophical
complement of his theology of faith.[28] Once more he called
attention to the relation between the knower's awareness of
his own connaturality to a known object his ability to grasp
the object's singular intelligibility. Unlike the pure spirits,

the human knower, who had no intuitive knowledge of his own essence, was not usually aware of his connaturality to a known object. Exceptional cases, of course, were found. A connoisseur of French life and culture, keenly aware of his sympathy for them, could savor with joy each one of their manifestations. He could respond to every expression of the French genius because he could see in it an "expression of himself." But the average Frenchman did not behave that way. Quite oblivious to his connaturality to the same objects and of his intrinsic sympathy toward them, he simply took them for granted and looked on them in an external, impersonal sort of way. Unable to "see himself in them," he could not enter into their unique intelligibility.[29]

This observation, Rousselot believed, had considerable significance for our understanding of the judgment. In St. Thomas's metaphysics of knowledge the judgment was an "apperceptive synthesis." To become aware of himself as a knower, man had first to abstract a universal form from a sensible image and then place the synthesis of universal form and singular object over against himself in the affirmation of the judgment. The act of human knowledge, in other words, was a continuous process of vital unification in which the intentional form of *species* of the sensible object was first "impressed" on the knower's "possible intellect" by the operation of his "active intellect." Only then could the knower "express himself" in the mental "word" of the judgment. His mind became able to "express *itself*" in its act of knowledge because the *species* "impressed" on it had made the mind itself ontologically like the object known in the mental word of the affirmation.[30] The *species impressa* in St. Thomas's metaphysics of knowledge produced an "enlightening sympathization of the mind."[31]

The whole act of knowledge in that mind was an uninterrupted immanent activity comparable to the vital "flower" of the "flower," and as the flower in the living plant could not be separated from the plant's immanent activity of "flower," the unified mental "synopsis" of the concept could not be separated from the unifying "apperceptive synthesis" accomplished in the living act of knowledge. It followed then that the nature and value of the dynamic process of cognition could not be determined by a static analysis of its product, the object represented in the concept.[32] The judgment was a dynamic process of unification whose grasp of the real was conditioned by the connaturality and love of the living, thinking mind, the sympathetic love of an abstractive human intelligence for the sensible object whose intentional form had been "impressed" upon it, and the love of that same intellect for the infinite being toward which its natural activity of unification tended as its last end. For, as Rousselot had already said in *L'Intellectualisme de Saint Thomas*, the intellect was the faculty of the real only because it was the faculty of the divine.[33]

Nonetheless, Rousselot agreed with Gardeil that the medium through which the human mind knew reality was the abstract idea of being drawn from sense experience. In St. Thomas's metaphysics man's essence was a form received in the matter which individuated it. Because the angel's essence was a pure form, the angel could "express *itself*" in knowing a pure form, either the form of another angel or the "quasi-exemplary" form the material *species* produced immediately in its mind by God.[34] But, as a form united to matter, man could "express *himself*" only through an intentional form received and spatialized by the matter which individuated it. This was the universal concept whose content had to be restored to the sensible singular, through its "concretion" by the mind's "conversion to the phantasm" in the judgment. Since man had no intuitive grasp of his own essence, as the angel did, his mind could know other essences only through its universal concepts. Of its nature, the mind of a form received in matter, as Rousselot said, "renders abstract everything it touches."[35]

In St. Thomas's metaphysics of knowledge then, the universal essence of a corporeal thing *(ens concretum quidditati materiali)*, which Rousselot called "the form of the thing," was the proper formal object of the human mind and the medium through which it knew every singular essence, including man's own. Therefore, man's knowledge of spiritual reality, even of his own soul, had to come to him indirectly and by analogy from his knowledge of the material objects known through the "category of the thing," or the "category of being."[36] Rousselot differed from Gardeil and Maritain, however, in his manner of defending Thomas's analogous knowledge of divine and spiritual reality against the charge of invalidity brought against it by Kantian idealism.

It was true that man's discursive intellect could know an object only by "synthesizing its content" from the data of sense experience, and it was also true that man, as a form received in matter, could have no intuitive grasp of any spiritual essence. That did not mean, however, that we should follow Kant's recommendation and limit the range of our speculative knowledge to the objects of Kant's phenomenal world of space and time. For man's activity of "unifying a object" was carried out by a mind whose ultimate end was intuitive union with infinite reality, and whose natural propensity therefore was to "place its synthesized objects in the real," unless awareness of an obvious contradiction prevented it from doing so.[37] In man's discursive intellect, the mind's natural finality took the place of angelic intuition in moving it to affirm the real existence of its objects.

Nor indeed was an intellectual intuition of a spiritual essence required, as Kant had claimed, to justify the speculative intellect's affirmation of its *possibility*. For, even though the human mind had no intuitive grasp of the identity between a universal essence and its singular subject, it had to *affirm* that identity in any judgment of reality. For, in order to affirm the reality of its objects, the human mind had to refer a universal to its singular subject by the "conversion to the phantasm," the process of "concretion" performed in every human judgment. That was why every abstracted essence that fell under the "categories" of "being" or "thing" had to contain within itself the reference to an indefinite subject, *hoc aliquid*.[38] It followed then that, in its very abstraction of being, the human mind also *affirmed* implicitly the identity of an essence with its concrete subject even though it could not *see* that identity in an intuition.

When therefore the human mind reflected on its activity of tending constantly toward an ever more perfect unification of its knowledge under the category of being, it became aware that it was a drive to develop itself into an intellect so perfectly unified that it could finally *see* the identity of subject and object fully and immediately in an intuition. Such a mind, however, had to be the mind of a pure form, freed from the constraints of matter and capable of grasping its own essence in an intuition. The drive of the human mind, Rousselot argued, was therefore *a natural drive to become an angel*.[39] In that case, pure spiritual reality was no more contradictory than the living process of thought which demanded it as the condition of possibility for its own progressive activity of unification. Contrary to Kant's contention then, the speculative intellect could know that finite spiritual reality is positively possible.

The same reflection would reveal the positive possibility of infinite spiritual reality. For, in its primordial judgment of reality the mind affirmed that an object *is*. Possible being, which could be known as such only through its relation to an existing being, depended on that primordial judgment for the appreciation of its own secondary intelligibility. But, in its primary judgment of existence, the mind *affirmed* the identity between a concrete essence and its existence without *seeing* that identity in an intuition.[40] Nevertheless, in affirming that identity, it was implicitly affirming the intelligibility of that union between essence and existence and hence also its relation to a mind capable of knowing it. Contained in the mind's primordial judgment of existence then was yet another affirmation. If there was a mind capable of knowing *all* reality, it would certainly know *that*.[41] Such a mind however would have to be the mind which knew the concrete existence of every actual existent by knowing its own unlimited existence. It would have to be, in other words, the divine mind. Hence the positive possibility of God was demanded by the drive of the human speculative intellect as the ground of its primordial judgment of existence.

Like Gardeil and Maritain therefore, Rousselot overcame Kant's objections against the human mind's ability to know God and spiritual reality through the analogy of being. Like them too, he insisted upon the necessity of the abstract notion of being for the human mind's knowledge of reality. But, whereas Gardeil and Maritain had based their realistic epistemology on the abstract notion of being itself, Rousselot grounded his on the concrete finality of the mind vitally operative in the twofold synthesis of the judgment: the "concretative synthesis" through which a universal essence was restored to its singular subject, and the "affirmative synthesis" in which the composite of universal form and singular subject was affirmed *to be* in the mind's primordial judgment of existence.[42]

Rousselot's Theology of Faith.

The metaphysics of knowledge which Rousselot had worked out in his philosophical articles provided the framework for his theology of faith. In *Les Yeux de la Foi*, Rousselot used it to show how, in every instance, the act of saving faith could be reasonable without sacrificing its free and supernatural character.[43] This was the same problem with which, as we recall, Gardeil had to grapple in his Dominican theology of faith.

If his act of faith were to be reasonable, the prospective believer had to possess convincing evidence that a truth had been revealed by God and that he was morally obliged to assent to it. But if, in order to make such a reasonable act of faith, the prospective believer had first to possess that evidence, how could his subsequent assent of faith retain its freedom?[44] Furthermore, if both the fact of revelation and man's moral obligation to assent to its content had to be knowable by the natural reason, to which apologetic arguments were directed, in order for a reasonable act of faith to be made, on what basis could it be claimed that the *subsequent* act of faith must be an *essentially supernatural act*? And indeed how could such a reasonable act of faith be in the power of the majority of Christians? Few Christians had the education required to appreciate scientific apologetic arguments and, for that reason, most Christians were never asked to reflect critically on the evidence which justified their assent of faith.[45]

St. Thomas's metaphysics of knowledge, Rousselot argued, would solve the set of problems connected with the act of faith. Rather than analyzing the believer's movement to faith into a set of discrete judgments and decisions on the level of *ratio* (reasoning), St. Thomas's metaphysics looked on it as a single uninterrupted movement on the level of *intellectus* (understanding). It was an "apperceptive synthesis," and the influence of connaturality and love operative in the "apperceptive synthesis" could account for the reasonableness and freedom of the act of faith.[46]

The metaphysics of *intellectus* and connaturality could explain why the act of faith was both reasonable and free precisely because it was supernatural. *Intellectus* was the mental function of immediate insight which provided discursive *ratio* with its first principles. It could be seen at work in the scientist's immediate "leap" from observed facts to general laws in the forming of his hypotheses. In his observed facts the scientist grasped the *clue* to his general laws in an intuitive act of *intellectus*. The clue then was prior to the law because it led to it. Yet, in another sense, the law was prior to the clue, since, only in the light of the general law, could the clue be seen as a clue and its significance in the law's general pattern be recognized. Unlike discursive *ratio*, *intellectus* grasped whole intelligible patterns in a moment of insight. Facts could be observed but they did not become clues until the flash of intuition took place in which the law was grasped.[47]

The power of *intellectus*, unlike Cartesian reason, varied in different knowers. Two scientists, looking for the same law, might examine the same set of data. In an instant, one might see the law while the other remained in ignorance of it. The objects remained the same but one observer had ac-

quired the power to see the intelligible pattern in the observed facts while the other had not. The difference between
the two scientists then was not a difference of *objects seen* but
of *eyes to see*.[48]

That difference was most significant for the theology of
faith. Through the influence of the infused virtue of faith,
the eye of *intellectus* could be elevated to the supernatural
order, made connatural to it, and infused with sympathetic
love toward it. Then it would be an *intellectus* capable of entering into a pattern of intelligibility which lay beyond the
grasp of an unelevated *intellectus*. Through the influence of
the supernatural habit of faith infused into it by God, the
human mind could then assent to the truth of revelation in a
supernatural act of faith. That act, however, had to be a reasonable one. Hence the believer who made it had also to
know that it could be justified by some fact in the world
accessible to his natural experience. It mattered little what
that concrete fact might be as long as it was a fact, which the
elevated *intellectus* could recognize as *a clue* which indicated
that a given truth had been revealed by God.[49] Elevated intuitive knowledge could recognize such a clue in a very simple
natural fact because, thanks to its connaturality to the supernatural order, it could grasp the higher pattern of intelligibility in which the clue and the revealed doctrine were liked
to one another. In other words, the act of faith was reasonable precisely because it was supernatural. Moved by connatural sympathy, the *intellectus* of the individual believer
could grasp the connection between a singular clue and a
revealed doctrine, a connection known perhaps only to the
believer himself and God. Where others saw nothing, he saw
the link in an act of insight because his elevated *intellectus*
had been given the eyes of faith. Enlightened by sympathetic
love, *intellectus* could grasp the unique intelligibility of the
singular.

Furthermore, the act of faith was reasonable because it
was free. The will could not only command the intellect to
turn its attention to a fact, the influence of the will could also
affect the way in which the intellect perceived it. Love could

both blind the intellect and give it new eyes to see. The sympathy which sprang from connaturality enable the knower to "enter into" an object. An object was known because a knower "expressed *himself*" in it. A new love then, a new "sympathy" in the knower, which enabled him to "enter into" a range of objects "closed" to him before, could open his intellect to a new world of being. The new love of an intellect elevated by grace and charity could give that intellect a new formal object and make it a cognitive faculty of an essentially higher order.[50]

The interrelation of love and knowledge could be seen in the "apperceptive synthesis" of faith. A man who was not yet justified could be drawn by God to the Christian faith. In that case, if he were to come upon a fact in the natural order which could become a clue to the truth of Christian revelation, his encounter with it would occur under the influence of grace. It would be a call from God to choose a new life addressed to the prospective convert's freedom. It could therefore be either accepted or rejected. Should it be accepted, however, the free choice of a life pleasing to God would bring the grace of justification to its chooser, and with justification would come as well the infused virtues of faith, hope, and charity.[51]

Elevated by grace, enlightened by faith, and moved by charity, the convert's intellect, through its sympathy with the supernatural order, could now see the connection between a fact of natural experience and the divine revelation of Christianity. The fact would have become a clue. Intellect and will worked reciprocally on one another in the "apperceptive synthesis" of faith. For, unless the will freely chose a life pleasing to God, the intellect would not be enlightened by the light of faith. Nevertheless each faculty did its own proper work. The will chose a life. The intellect saw a clue. Still, by choosing to accept a freely given grace, the justified convert had acquired a new nature, and the new nature gave him the power to see with the eyes of faith. In one and the same movement the will made the intellect's vision possible, and the vision of the intellect justified the choice of the will.[52]

The intellect could see the clue only because the will had freely chosen to accept God's grace.

Nor was this assent of the intellect in any way illegitimate because it had been made under the influence of the will. Granted that the will's love for a particular good could indeed blind the intellect and render its assent illegitimate, that was not the case in the mind's free assent of faith.[53] For the only reason why the mind could make any assent at all under the "category of being" was that the intellect, by its very nature, was a "faculty of the divine" whose ultimate end was intentional union with the Infinite First Truth. As St. Thomas had shown in his metaphysics of knowledge, the full perfection of the intellect was reached in its intuitive grasp of God under the "light of glory" in the Beatific Vision. The free choice of the will, which expanded the range of the intellect, through the supernatural light of faith, led to the intellect's highest functioning in its own proper order as an intellect. That free choice did not blind the intellect. On the contrary, it gave the intellect "the eyes to see."

Later research on Rousselot's unpublished writings has shown that Rousselot might have made significant revisions in his philosophy of knowledge and in his theology of faith, if death had not ended his career in 1915. Between 1908 and 1914, however, he made a major contribution to the tradition of St. Thomas. His Thomistic realism, which highlighted the role of *intellectus* and the dynamism of the mind while downplaying the importance of the concept, was very different from the Thomism of Gardeil, Garrigou-Lagrange, and Maritain. Together with the Thomism of Joseph Maréchal, it would create the tradition in Neo-Thomism known today as Transcendental Thomism.

Notes

1. *L'Intellectualisme de Saint Thomas* (Paris: Beauchesne, 1924), p. xviii.

2. *L'Intellectualisme*, pp. 144-47.

3. John M. McDermott, S.J. "Un Inédit de Rousselot: Idéalisme et Thomisme," *Archives de Philosophie*, 42 (1979), p. 92.

4. *Pour L'Histoire du Problème de l'Amour au Moyen-Age* (Münster: Aschendorff, 1908).

5. *L'Intellectualisme*, pp. 42-43.

6. *L'Intellectualisme*, pp. 39-40.

7. *L'Intellectualisme*, pp. 32-36.

8. *Problème de l'Amour*, pp. 3, 12-13, 30-32.

9. *L'Intellectualisme*, pp. 36-40.

10. *L'Intellectualisme*, p. v.

11. *Problème de l'Amour*, pp. 12-14, 20-21, 29-32.

12. *Problème de l'Amour*, pp. 19-20; *L'Intellectualisme*, pp. 29-32.

13. *Problème de l'Amour*, pp. 30-32.

14. *L'Intellectualisme*, pp. 226-29.

15. *L'Intellectualisme*, pp. iii, 38-39.

16. "Métaphysique Thomiste et Critique de la Connaissance," *Revue Néoscholastique de Philosophie* 17 (1910), pp. 483-84.

17. *L'Intellectualisme*, pp. 56-57.

18. *L'Intellectualisme*, pp. 20, 44-46, 224.

19. "Amour Spirituel et Synthèse Apperceptive," *Revue de Philosophie* 16 (1910), p. 235.

20. *L'Intellectualisme*, pp. 17-19.

21. *L'Intellectualisme*, pp. 26-30.

22. *L'Intellectualisme*, pp. 39-40.

23. The second chapter of the second part of *L'Intellectualisme* is devoted to the concept as a substitute for intuition.

24. *L'Intellectualisme*, pp. 81-89.

25. *L'Intellectualisme*, pp. 94-95.

26. *L'Intellectualisme*, pp. 143-44.

27. *L'Intellectualisme*, pp. 108-32.

28. "Amour Spirituel et Synthèse Apperceptive," *Revue de Philosophie* 16 (1910), pp. 225-40; "L'Etre et l'Esprit," *Revue de Philosophie* 16 (1910), pp. 561-74; "Métaphysique Thomiste et Critique de la Connaissance," *Revue Néoscholastique de Philosophie*, 17 (1910), pp. 476-509.

29. "Métaphysique Thomiste," pp. 568-69.

30. "L'Etre et l'Esprit," pp. 561-63.

31. "L'Etre et l'Esprit," p. 563.

32. "Amour Spirituel," pp. 237-38.

33. *L'Intellectualisme*, p. v.

34. "Métaphysique Thomiste," p. 484; "Amour Spirituel," pp. 229-30; "L'Etre et l'Esprit, p. 563; *L'Intellectualisme*, pp. 17-19.

35. "Métaphysique Thomiste," pp. 484-85; "L'Etre et l'Esprit," pp. 564-66.

36. "Métaphysique Thomiste," pp. 487-89.

37. Rousselot was influenced in his philosophical articles by Joseph Maréchal's article, "A Propos du Sentiment de Présence chez les Profanes et chez les Mystiques," *Revue des Questions Scientifiques*, pp. 64-65 (1908-09). Repr. in Joseph Maréchal, S.J., *Etudes sur la Psychologie des Mystiques*, I (Paris: Desclée De Brouwer, 1938), pp. 65-168. Maréchal explained the mind's propensity to place its objects in reality by its tendency to God as its natural end.

38. "Métaphysique Thomiste," pp. 495-97.

39. "Métaphysique Thomiste," pp. 496-97.

40. "Métaphysique Thomiste," pp. 497-98.

41. "Métaphysique Thomiste," pp. 497-99.

42. Rousselot himself did not use this terminology as later Neo-Thomists did. Nevertheless it is faithful to his thought.

43. "Les Yeux de la Foi," *Recherches de Science Religieux* 1 (1910), pp. 241-59, 444-75.

44. "Les Yeux de la Foi," pp. 444.

45. "Les Yeux de la Foi," pp. 247-48.

46. "Les Yeux de la Foi," pp. 251-52.

47. "Les Yeux de la Foi," pp. 251-54.

48. "Les Yeux de la Foi," pp. 258-59.

49. "Les Yeux de la Foi," pp. 256-57.

50. "Les Yeux de la Foi," pp. 448-51.

51. See Henri Holstein, S.J., "Le Théologien de la Foi," *Recherches de Science Religieux* 53 (1965), pp. 86-125, esp. pp. 119-25.

52. "Les Yeux de la Foi," pp. 450-51, pp. 457-58.

53. "Les Yeux de la Foi," pp. 452-56.

54. See John M. McDermott, S.J., *Love and Understanding: The Relation Between the Will and the Intellect in Pierre Rousselot's Christological Vision* (Rome: Università Gregoriana Editrice, 1982), pp. 188-90, 224-28.

Chapter Six
Joseph Maréchal

Joseph Maréchal was the Neo-Scholastic with whom the origin of Transcendental Thomism has been most closely associated. Unlike his fellow Jesuit, Pierre Rousselot, Maréchal made his reputation as a philosopher. His interests, however, were not confined to that field. Before he began to teach philosophy he had taken his doctorate in biology at the University of Louvain as a preparation for the research in psychology which led to his *Studies in the Psychology of the Mystics*.[1] He was an expert in the history of philosophy with an exact and sympathetic understanding of Kantian and Post-Kantian idealism which few Neo-Scholastics could rival. His comparative study of Kant and St. Thomas had convinced him that the opposition between Kantian idealism and St. Thomas's realism, which most Neo-Scholastics considered to be irreconcilable, need not be the inevitable result of the use of Kant's Transcendental Method.

Despite Maréchal's recognized ability, however, the University of Louvain never invited him to join its faculty, and his teaching career between the two World Wars was spent at Jesuit Houses of Study, first in Louvain and later in the nearby suburb of Eegenhoven.[2] His international reputation was due to the appreciation of his work shown by his own religious order, particularly in Belgium and France, and to his five-volume masterpiece, *Le Point de Départ de la Métaphysique*.[3]

As the title of his major work made plain, Maréchal's main concern was the epistemological grounding of a realistic metaphysics of being. This was the same concern which had moved both Blondel and the Dominican Thomists to develop their diverse philosophies of knowledge and being in the last decades of the nineteenth century and the opening decade of the twentieth. The position against which both of these philosophies were directed was the Kantian idealism which restricted the range of human knowledge to the phenomenal world of space and time. If Catholic theology was to retain a solid footing in reality, Kantian idealism would have to be overcome through a realistic epistemology which would both link the human mind to the extra-mental world and enable it to acquire genuine, though limited, speculative knowledge of God through the analogy of being.

Both the Dominican Thomists and Maritain grounded their immediate realism on the abstract idea of being. Both were aware of St. Thomas's use of *intellectus* and both appreciated the place of the metaphysics of final causality in St. Thomas's philosophy of the intellect and will. Nevertheless, it was the immediate contact of the intellect with reality through the abstract idea of being which was "the starting point of metaphysics" in their understanding of Thomism.

Under the influence of Maréchal, Rousselot had come to another conclusion. Every finite intellect was, by its very nature, a drive to Infinite Being. That was the fundamental reason why, although the content of its abstracted concepts was confined to the finite, contingent world of senses. The human intellect could affirm the reality of that content in its judgments under the necessary and universal law of being. The intellect was "the sense of the real," Rousselot had claimed in *L'Intellectualisme de Saint Thomas, because* it was "the sense of the divine."[4] The mind's tendency toward its last end, which penetrated the vital act of knowledge in every judgment, compelled the intellect by its very nature to refer the contingent objects of its concepts to God's Necessary Being as the goal of the mind's unending desire to know. Since every finite object known by the mind became a partial fulfillment of the mind's innate desire to know God, each one of them was caught up in the intellectual process which that desire had set in motion and inserted into the mind's ongoing tendency toward God.[5] In Maréchal's interpretation of St. Thomas, then, this implicit reference of every contingent object to God's Necessary Being in "the metaphysical affirmation" associated with every judgment—rather than the abstracted idea of being—was the realistic "starting point" in knowledge for St. Thomas's metaphysics.[6]

St. Thomas and Kant on Metaphysics.

Maréchal's understanding of the judgment as a vital reference of contingent objects to Necessary Being through the natural drive of the mind to God would play an important role in establishing the compatibility of Kant's transcendental method with Thomistic realism. There were many similarities, he observed, between the Kantian and the Thomistic approach to metaphysics. Despite their disagreement about its possibility, both Kant and St. Thomas shared the same conception of what metaphysics should be. For both of them a distinguishing characteristic of metaphysics was its strictly universal and necessary knowledge, the type of knowledge which Plato and Aristotle called *episteme* and which Kant and the German idealists called *Wissenschaft.*[7] The apodictic certitude of its conclusions therefore made metaphysics a science of an essentially higher order than the empirical science of Locke and Hume which laid claim to no more than probability. If metaphysics should prove to be speculatively valid, its universal concepts would yield knowledge of real essences—genuine possibles. Locke's empirical "nominal essences," on the other hand, could yield no knowledge of "what things really were." In company with St. Thomas, Descartes, and Spinoza, Kant believed that the necessary and universal synthesis of human knowledge, to which a speculative metaphysics should lead, must be grounded upon speculative knowledge of Absolute Being, the unitary ground of true knowledge and reality. He stood in opposition—again with Thomas and the Continental Rationalists—to the empiricists' theory of knowledge which would deprive metaphysics of any sort of legitimacy. Metaphysics for Kant had its origin in the subjective necessity which impelled the discursive mind to unify and ground its knowledge, and, in endeavoring to do so, the mind was driven to refer the objects of its necessary and universal judgments to the Absolutely Perfect Being as the unconditioned ground of their intelligible unity.

On the other hand, Kant did not agree wither with St. Thomas or the Continental Rationalists about the speculative validity of metaphysics. As an activity, metaphysics was indeed a subjective necessity of the mind. Nevertheless, the *a priori* conditions for the unification of discursive knowledge made a speculatively valid metaphysics impossible.

In order to have valid metaphysical knowledge, Kant asserted, the discursive mind would have to possess an immediate awareness of extra-mental—or, as Kant called it, *noumenal*—intelligibility. In other words, it must have an immediate intellectual intuition of intelligible being. Descartes had claimed that the discursive mind possessed an intellectual intuition of its own finite spiritual reality in the clear and distinct idea of the self as a thinking substance. He also claimed that it had an intellectual intuition of God's essence as a "real possible" in its clear and distinct idea of the Absolutely Perfect Being. St. Augustine was convinced that the finite mind had an intellectual intuition of its own contingent mobile reality and of the Changeless Light, the Necessary Truth, which ruled its judgments.

Kant's critique of knowledge, however, challenged the claim that the discursive mind could have an intellectual intuition either of its own finite contingent reality or of God's Infinite and Necessary Being. No object could become intelligible until it had been "constituted" as a phenomenal object through a preconscious process of unification. Only after it had been "unified" from the data of sense by the forms of sensibility and the categories of the understanding could a phenomenal object be "understood" and affirmed in the judgment. Like its multiple objects, the unitary subject pole of consciousness, to which the manifold world of objects "appeared," emerged into self-awareness only after a similar process of preconscious unification. The transcendental unity of apperception—Kant's phenomenal "I think"—was not and could never be identical with the real substantial self—Kant's "noumenal ego"—as Descartes's "thinking self" had been.

Furthermore, since Infinite Being was not one of the phenomenal spatiotemporal objects "constituted" in consciousness, the human mind could not possess the immediate knowledge of God's "real possibility" which Descartes claimed to have in his clear and distinct idea of the Absolutely Perfect Being. It followed then that the discursive mind could have neither of the intellectual intuitions required to justify a valid metaphysics. Metaphysics was legitimate as a subjective impulse of the mind to unify and ground its knowledge but it was not a legitimate source of knowledge about reality.[8]

Yet, as Maréchal observed, Thomas agreed with Kant that the human knower could have no intellectual intuition either of the soul's essential reality or of God's essence. For that very reason, Thomas had denied the validity of any argument for God's existence based on the mind's idea of God centuries before Descartes had proposed his celebrated argument for God's existence in his *Fifth Meditation*. In Thomas's philosophy of knowledge, the operation of the Aristotelian active intellect replaced the Augustinian "intuition" of the divine ideas as the ground of the universality and necessity of intellectual knowledge. Consequently, for Thomas as for Kant, the whole representative content of the mind's universal ideas was derived from the contingent spatiotemporal world of sense experience; and, for Thomas as for Kant, conceptual knowledge was the result of the mind's active construction of its content rather than of its passive intellectual intuition of an already given essence.[9] The objects represented in abstracted universals had to be unified, first on the level of sense and then on the level of the intellect, before their intelligibility could be formulated in the concept and their reality affirmed in the judgment. Therefore, for Thomas the proper object of the human mind was the essence of a material being *(ens concretum quidditate materiali)*, and nothing transcending the spatiotemporal world could be directly represented in its abstracted concepts.[10] Nevertheless, St. Thomas showed none of Kant's distrust of speculative metaphysics. In Thomas's philosophy of knowledge the human mind affirmed the reality of its objects under the necessary and universal law of being manifested in the principle of identify, and, despite the fact that the mind's proper object was the essence of material beings, it could arrive at indirect and imperfect knowledge of divine and spiritual reality through the analogy of being.[11]

Why this great difference in their attitude toward metaphysics in these two philosophers, whose philosophy of knowledge had so much in common and both of whom had denied the possibility of intellectual intuition in the discursive mind? Perhaps Thomas had simply shared the uncritical realism of the Middle Ages. Or, perhaps, on the other hand, he had observed some elements in the process of unifying and affirming phenomenal objects which Kant had failed to see. If the latter were true, it might justify Thomas's confidence in a realistic metaphysics and it might open up the possibility of linking Kant's approach to knowledge with a realistic metaphysics of being.

The Key to the Solution: The Transcendental Method.

The way to find out, Maréchal believed, was to apply to Thomas's metaphysics of knowledge the transcendental method which Kant had used in his *Critique of Pure Reason* to uncover the *a priori* conditions of possibility for speculative knowledge.[12] And, after his historical study of ancient and mediæval philosophy of knowledge in the first and second volumes of *Le Point de Départ de la Métaphysique* and his remarkably exact and sympathetic account of Kant's critical idealism in its third volume, Maréchal undertook an extensive in-depth analysis of Thomas's grounding of metaphysical knowledge in the difficult and controversial fifth volume of his major work.[13]

Despite the sinuous complexity of its exposition, the thrust of Maréchal's fifth volume was clear enough. In essence, its aim was to find the answer to two questions. What was there in Thomas's metaphysics of knowledge which justified the Angelic Doctor's claim that the discursive mind could legitimately place the objects of its judgments in reality under the universal law of being, even though, as Thomas himself admitted, it could have no intellectual intuition of any essence, even of its own? Why was it that, although both Thomas and Kant both claimed that the content of the discursive reason's conceptual objects must be unified by the human mind from the disparate data of sense intuition, Thomas's discursive intellect could unify these objects under the all-embracing, transcendental and analogous unity of being whereas their unification by Kant's discursive reason was limited to the univocal and categorical unity of his phenomenal world of space and time?

If a satisfactory answer to these two questions could be found, then the restrictions of Kantian idealism might be overcome. Thomas's philosophy of knowledge might provide the grounding for a realistic epistemology, and it might also vindicate the mind's speculative knowledge of God through the analogy of being. The starting point of the realistic metaphysics which Catholic theology required to validate its claims against the objections of Kantianism, empiricism, and Modernism might have been found.

Maréchal therefore proceeded to direct Kant's set of fundamental questions to St. Thomas. What, as a matter of fact, are the preconscious conditions of possibility required for the unification and affirmation of the interrelated set of objects which reflective reason finds already given in its consciousness? Do these conditions for the possibility of an object's appearance turn out to be a number of "faculties" or functions of conscious unification? If so, are they found both on the level of sense and on the level of intellect? Can critical reflection go further and establish that the "faculties" required to "mould" or "unify" the objects which actually appear in consciousness from the disorganized data of raw experience are also the conditions of possibility for the *appearance of any object of consciousness whatsoever?* In that case, it would be impossible for an object to be given in consciousness unless its content had already been unified by them. It would follow then that any attempt to affirm any object while denying the existence of these *a priori* conditions of its possibility would be logically impossible. Such a denial would be self-refuting since it would entail a logical contradiction.

Kant's critical reflection on the objects given in consciousness, guided by this systematic set of questions about the *a priori*, or preconscious, conditions of possibility for their appearance, is what was meant by his transcendental method. He compared the method to the working out of a "transcendental logic" which laid out in order the *a priori* conditions of its possibility logically entailed in speculative reason's affirmation of any object. The progressive steps of this "logic" established that the singular sensible forms of space and time, the universal categories of the understanding, and the transcendental unity of apperception had to be co-affirmed with logical necessity in every objective judgment.

Although Kant was a critical idealist and St. Thomas a realist in his epistemology, Maréchal believed that a comparative study of their accounts of the unification and the affirmation of an object should be made. St. Thomas's account, of course, was a metaphysical one, given in terms of his Aristotelian philosophy of the four causes. Kant's "moulders" or "unifiers" of his conscious object had been no more than logical functions of consciousness. Thomas's "unifiers" of his objects, on the other hand, were real Aristotelian faculties, accidental powers of knowing—inhering either in the soul or in the animated body—ordered to their proper object as their final cause and through which a substantial human agent acted.

Nevertheless, Maréchal attempted to work out a "metaphysical critique" of Thomas's conscious object drawing upon Thomas's metaphysics of knowledge but following the order and method of Kant's "transcendental logic." In this way he hoped to make the direct and precise comparison between Kant's critical idealism and Thomas's metaphysical realism through which the significant similarities and differences in the two accounts of the unification and affirmation of an object could come to light.

Abstraction vs. Intellectual Intuition.

Most of the fifth volume of *Le Point de Départ de la Métaphysique* was devoted to this "metaphysical critique" of the object of knowledge in terms of St. Thomas's philosophy of being.[13] Maréchal's exposition of St. Thomas's metaphysical "transcendental logic" turned first to the role played by the external and internal faculties of sense in the structuring of the organized sense image.[14] Then it took up the cooperation of the imagination and the active intellect in the abstraction of the universal concept.[15] Finally, it distinguished between the diverse functions assigned to the "concretative synthesis" and the "ontological affirmation" in the act of the judgment.[16] Maréchal called his readers' attention to the similarities between Kant's unification of the sensible object through the *a priori* forms of space and time and Thomas's metaphysical account of formative role of the exterior and interior senses in the organization of the image. The functioning of these sense faculties was predetermined by the natural tendency of their activity toward their own proper object as its pre-given final cause. Other similarities could be observed on the higher level of the understanding. Kant accounted for the concrete determination of his objects through the application of the universal *a priori* categories of the understanding to singular sense data by the schemata of the imagination. Thomas explained the abstraction of the universal concept from the sense image by the cooperation of the imagination and the active intellect; and the mind's knowledge of singular objects was explained by its "concretization" of its abstract concepts through its "return to the phantasm," i.e. the singular sense image, in the "concretative synthesis" of the judgment.

Thus, for Thomas as for Kant, the unified content of the mind's concepts was accounted for through the "determinations" imposed on the "matter" of sense data through a progressive series of cognitional "forms" imposed on a "prime matter" of sensation by an ascending series of *a priori* functions of unification operative on the levels of both sense and intellect. And again, for Thomas as for Kant, no real object could be known until the abstract content of the mind's universal concepts has been reunited through the cooperation of the imagination with the concrete singulars of the spatiotemporal world. For both philosophers *the whole represen-tative content of man's conceptual knowledge* was restricted to the world of space and time.[17]

In addition to the union of universal form and singular matter in the "concretative synthesis" of the judgment there was another element in St. Thomas's metaphysical analysis of knowledge to which Kant had not paid enough attention in his idealistic account of it. This was the all important part which Thomas assigned to final causality in securing the co-operation of sense and intellect in the unitary act of human knowledge.[18] The natural tendency of the human mind to-ward its own last end accounted for its ability to direct the activity of man's sensitive faculties in their tendency toward their own proper ends. The substantial form of man's Aris-totelian human nature was his intellectual soul, and, in Aristotle's metaphysics of the faculties, lower faculties were directed by a nature's higher, specific faculties in an Aristo-telian agent's unified tendency towards the proper good of its whole nature. The proper good of human nature was its union with infinite being toward which the intellect, as man's defining faculty, tended. The mind's tendency toward its last end, however, did more than enable the intellect to direct the activities of the sense faculties in their formal structur-ing of an object of knowledge.[19] The mind's own activity of unification in the formation of its concepts was a partial moment in its vital aspiration to intentional unity with the infinite plenitude of being as its final end. That was why, although the unified content of its abstracted concepts was restricted to the categorical unity of the finite world of space and time, the discursive mind could synthesize its finite world of objects under the transcendental unity of being.[20] For in-finite being, as the end which specified the mind's activity, made the unrestricted "form" of being itself, rather than the restricted "form" of spatiotemporal being, the determining "form" of the activity through which the mind progressively unified the objects of its knowledge. Because the mind's knowledge of contingent objects in the judgment was no more than a partial satisfaction of an unrestricted questioning drive, which carried man's inquiring intellect beyond any contingent object, the discursive mind could affirm each one of its limited objects with the unlimited necessity of the principle of identity. For, even though every limited known object gave partial satisfaction to the mind at the instant of its affirmation in the judgment, the same contingent object immediately became the source of further questions. Caught up once more in the movement of the mind's insatiable desire to know, the contingent object of the judgment was then related, as an intermediate end to the infinite and necessary goal of the mind's natural finality.[21]

That essential reference of the mind's contingent objects to absolutely necessary being as the goal of the mind's finality took place in what Maréchal called "the ontological affirmation."[22] The finality of the mind, which justified the "ontological affirmation" in every judgment, was the reason why St. Thomas was convinced that the abstraction of the concept through the cooperative activity of sense and intellect, together with the mind's affirmation of conceptual objects in the judgment, could perform the function of grounding a realistic metaphysics of being which the Platonists had assigned to intellectual intuition. Every finite conditioned object was grounded in an unconditioned Absolute. For its participation in God's self-grounding intelligibility was the source of the contingent intelligibility through which it could give partial satisfaction to the mind's unlimited desire to know.[23]

Therefore, Kant had not discovered a significant *a priori* condition for the possibility of knowledge which Thomas, in his mediæval naiveté, had failed to notice. The opposite was true. Kant had taken the Aristotelian metaphysics of form and matter as the model for his *a priori* formation of conscious objects by his preconscious functions of unification. He had failed to see that, although form and matter might suffice to account for the static intelligibility of a stable object, more was required to account for the dynamic intelligibility of a progressive movement. As Aristotle saw, movements, as intelligible tendencies, could be specified only by their goal or end. Formal causality was not sufficient to explain them. Final causality was also needed.

But, as Kant himself should have seen, the "formation" or "constitution" of a conscious object was a movement, an intelligible, goal-directed process; and that movement — through which every object in consciousness was progressively constituted — demanded the influence of an existing Absolute Being upon it as its final cause to account for its intelligibility. In that case the influence of an actually existing God on the moving mind as the final cause of its activity was one of the *a priori* conditions of possibility for the formation of any object in discursive consciousness. If Kant had been thorough enough and consistent enough in the use of his own transcendental method, He would not have remained a critical idealist. As St. Thomas had done, he would have embraced a metaphysical realism. Kant's idealism was not the result of the transcendental method itself. It was the result of Kant's lack of consistency in his use of it.

Maréchal's Thomistic Correction of Kant.

Maréchal endeavored to justify this claim in the much briefer "transcendental critique" of the conscious object which he undertook at the conclusion of the fifth volume of *Le Point de Départ de la Métaphysique*. Through this critique Maréchal hoped to go in Kant's door and come out his own. In other words, using Kant's own transcendental method, he intended to inquire systematically into the *a priori* conditions of possibility for the appearance of an object in consciousness. He would not make the claim, which St. Thomas had made in his metaphysical critique, that conscious objects were a valid source of knowledge about "noumenal," or extra-mental, reality. Neither, however, would he prejudge the outcome of his inquiry at its start by assuming that Kant was right and that the objects of consciousness could give valid knowledge only of Kant's intramental or phenomenal world.

The approach taken to the conscious object at the beginning of an unprejudiced critique of knowledge should be a strictly "precisive" one. Objects should be regarded neutrally in their state of "givenness." No commitment—either to idealism or realism—should be made until the evidence revealed in the critical inquiry itself could justify it.

Kant's own conclusion in *The Critique of Pure Reason* had been that the objects given in consciousness must be "phenomenal" objects. His reason for coming to it had been that the only objects which could "appear" to discursive consciousness were the objects which had already been "preformed" from the data of raw sensation by the *a priori* sensible forms of space and time and the *a priori* categories of the understanding. What an extra-mental sensible reality might be like before its "transformation" by the *a priori* functions of consciousness must remain forever an insoluble mystery. The nature of sensible reality would always be an "unknown x" for discursive reason. The real nature of spiritual reality would remain equally mysterious, since discursive reason lacked the power of intellectual intuition required to know it. Consequently the world of organized objects which appeared to the "I think" of consciousness had to be Kant's purely phenomenal world of space and time.

A number of Kant's own admissions, however, could tell against this idealistic conclusion. His own argument for the legitimacy of metaphysics, directed against the empiricists, had been that metaphysics was required by a subjective necessity of discursive reason. The intrinsic dynamism of discursive consciousness moved it to unify its objects and attempt to ground their conditioned contingency in the unconditioned necessity of Absolute Being. In the *Transcendental Dialectic* of Kant's *Critique of Pure Reason,* the infinite Absolutely Perfect Being was claimed to be a "regulative ideal" of discursive reason on these very grounds. Discursive reason was impelled to do more than simply "organize" its objects through the preconscious functioning of sensible forms and intellectual categories; it was driven on to relate its world of organized objects on the conscious level in increasingly extensive and ever more thoroughly grounded scientific systems. The ideal toward which the discursive mind was im-

pelled to move by that necessary subjective impulse was sa-
tiating knowledge of God's infinite and self-grounding intelligibility as the Absolutely Perfect Being. It could be no less.
For no finite and contingent object and no world of finite
and contingent objects could satisfy the mind's unquench-
able desire to unify and ground its knowledge. The discursive mind's insatiable "urge to question" meant that its quest
for answers must reach beyond the limits of any finite world
of objects. Knowledge of God them, as Infinite Unconditioned Intelligibility, was the ideal goal toward which the
activity of metaphysical inquiry was constantly tending.
Only God's unlimited self-grounding intelligibility could
satisfy the desire which provoked it by giving the ultimate answer to its questions.

For Kant, however, God, known by discursive reason,
had to remain an asymptote, a "purely regulative ideal." For
a discursive reason, deprived of intellectual intuition, the very
possibility of God in the extra-mental world of noumenal
reality was an open question. God was neither one of the
finite objects appearing in the phenomenal world of space
and time, nor, in the Kantian critique of knowledge, was He
one of the *a priori* conditions of an object's "constitution,"
one of the conditions, in other words, whose simultaneous
affirmation was logically demanded by the affirmation of any
phenomenal object. Thus, as far as speculative reason was
concerned, God could be either possible or impossible. The
mind's longing to know God justified and directed the legitimate activity of metaphysical thinking. But neither metaphysics nor any other form of speculative knowledge, could
say anything about God's real existence.

This, however, Maréchal objected, was a serious mis-
take. The occasion for it had been Kant's inconsistency in
constituting the objects in his phenomenal world in a purely
static manner, even though, according to the logic of his
method, the "formation" of these objects should have been
recognized as a progressive dynamic process. Looked at stati-
cally, Kant's objects of consciousness could be explained in
terms of a set of immobile forms imposed on the formless

matter of sensation. In that case, of course, the objects of consciousness would have to be purely "phenomenal" and Kant's critical idealism would be justified.

But, even if these forms were taken to be no more than purely logical functions of unification, as Kant had considered them to be in his *Critique of Pure Reason*, and as Maréchal intended to treat them in his own "transcendental critique," they could not be considered as isolated, immobile "forms," with no intelligible relation to one another. Moving forward from the forms of space and time through the categories and their schemata to the transcendental unity of apperception, Kant's conscious "I think," these formal elements could make sense only in their dynamic relation to each other as orderly successive stages in a single dynamic process of formation. Thus, even in terms of Kant's purely logical conception of his functions of unification, the *a priori* constitution of his conscious object had to be seen as a dynamic tendential process, an intelligible movement; and the intelligibility of a movement could come only from its final cause, the end which specified it as an appetite.[25]

Kant himself had conceded that the order of ends was not a phenomenal but rather a noumenal one. Even without that telling admission, however, Maréchal was convinced that the necessary inclusion of final causality among the conditions of possibility for the *a priori* constitution of an object was enough to show that Kant's transcendental method must lead to realism. An object's appearance in consciousness was the result of a preconscious *a priori* drive to unify and affirm an object of knowledge. The same inner drive continued and, as Kant pointed out in the *Transcendental Dialectic,* impelled the mind to unify and ground its knowledge on the conscious level in its ceaseless tendency toward God, as a "transcendental ideal" of speculative reason. Therefore, the uninterrupted movement of consciousness in both its *a priori* constitution of its objects and in its scientific unification of them on the conscious level manifested itself to be the effect of a single intelligible tendency whose ultimate and specifying end was knowledge of God's infinite and necessary being.[26]

In that case, the question about God's possibility could no longer be, as Kant had thought, an open one. For no final cause, whose influence specified an intelligible movement towards it, could itself be impossible. If it were, it would be absolute non-being, or, in other words, sheer nothing. But a tendency toward sheer nothing would be no tendency at all.[27] It could not be the intelligible motion required to constitute a conscious object. God's possibility, moreover, required His actual existence, since no self-grounding being could be dependent on another being as the cause of its existence.

God's actual existence then, as the goal of the intelligible process involved in every conscious object's constitution, had to be included among the *a priori* conditions of possibility for its appearance. Therefore to affirm any object whatsoever and to deny God's real existence would involve a logical contradiction.[28] It followed then that, once Kant's transcendental method was employed with the requisite thoroughness and consistence, it led with logical necessity to the metaphysical realism of Thomas rather than to the critical idealism of Kant.

Maréchal's dialogue with Kant in *Le Point de Départ de la Métaphysique* led to two important breaks with the other schools of Neo-Thomism. Maréchal's metaphysical critique of the object justified the mind's hold on extra-mental reality through the dynamic reference of the mind's conceptual objects to God's necessary being which took place in the metaphysical affirmation of the judgment. Dominican and Maritainian Thomists, on the contrary, grounded the mind's knowledge of reality through an immediate intellectual contact with the real in the abstract transcendental concept of being. For Gilson, as we shall see, being was known through the mind's grasp of concrete contingent existence in its affirmation of a sensible singular object.

In his transcendental critique of the object, Maréchal had given his approval to Kant's subjective starting point for philosophy. A Thomistic critique of knowledge, he argued, could begin with a "precisive" approach to realism and idealism. It could then work its way from the world of phenomena into the world of real being through its consistent use of Kant's transcendental method. None of the other Neo-Thomists would sanction the validity of this approach to Thomistic epistemology.[29] Thus Thomists in the tradition of Maréchal and Rousselot were distinguished from other Neo-Thomists by the significant role which they assigned to the dynamism of the mind in grounding the validity of metaphysics. For Maréchal, as well as for Rousselot, the intellect was "the sense of the real" *precisely because* it was "the sense of the divine."[30]

Notes

1. *Etudes sur la Psychologie des Mystiques*, 2 vols. (Paris: Desclée De Brouwer, 1938).

2. Joseph Donceel, S.J., *A Maréchal Reader* (New York: Herder and Herder, 1970), p. xi. Donceel, a former student and personal friend of Maréchal, is one of the most reliable expositors of Maréchal's philosophy in the English speaking world. His *Reader*, a selection of crucial texts, linked together by his perceptive comments, is the most thorough presentation of *Le Point de Départ* to be found in English. Maréchal's major work has never been translated.

3. *Le Point de Départ de la Métaphysique: Leçons sur le Développement Historique et Théorique du Problème de la Connaissance*, 5 vols. (Paris: Desclée De Brouwer, 1944-49).

4. *L'Intellectualisme de Saint Thomas*, p. v.

5. See Maréchal's article, "Le Dynamisme Intellectuelle dans la Connaissance Objective" in *Mélanges Joseph Maréchal*, 2 vols. (Paris: Desclée De Brouwer, 1950), v. 1, 75-101. (*Maréchal Reader*, pp. 244-50. Also *Le Point de Départ*, v. 5, pp. 305-15 (*Maréchal Reader*, pp. 149-53).

6. *Le Point de Départ*, v. 5, pp. 317-18. (*Maréchal Reader*, pp. 153-54).

7. See Maréchal's article, "Au Seuil de la Métaphysique: Abstraction ou Intuition?" in Mélanges Joseph Maréchal, pp. 102-80, esp. 104-07. (*Maréchal Reader*, pp. 235-244, esp. pp. 235-36).

8. "Abstraction ou Intuition?" in *Mélanges Joseph Maréchal,* pp. 145-49.

9. *Le Point de Départ,* v. 5, pp. 276-79, (*Maréchal Reader,* pp. 147-48.)

10. *Le Point de Départ,* v. 5, pp. 220-23.

11. *Le Point de Départ,* v. 5, pp. 257-59. (*Maréchal Reader,* pp. 144-45.)

12. *Le Point de Départ,* v. 5, pp. 47-71. (*Maréchal Reader,* pp. 66-88.)

13. The fifth volume, dealing with Kant's later philosophy and Post-Kantian idealism, was not yet finished at Maréchal's death. It was published posthumously.

13a. This critique runs from pages 81 to 504 of the fifth volume of *Le Point de Départ.* For a selection of significant texts from it see *A Maréchal Reader.*

14. *Le Point de Départ,* v. 5, pp. 131-84. (*Maréchal Reader,* pp. 116-25.)

15. *Le Point de Départ,* v. 5, pp. 185-223. (*Maréchal Reader,* pp. 125-43.)

16. *Le Point de Départ,* v. 5, pp. 281-315. (*Maréchal Reader,* pp. 149-53.)

17. *Le Point de Départ,* v. 5, pp. 298-304.

18. *Le Point de Départ,* v. 5, pp. 298-315. (*Maréchal Reader,* pp. 149-53.)

19. *Le Point de Départ,* v. 5, pp. 201-07. (*Maréchal Reader,* pp. 128-33.)

20. *Le Point de Départ,* v. 5, pp. 257-59, 276-79, 296-98. (*Maréchal Reader,* pp. 114-45, 147-49.)

21. *Le Point de Départ,* v. 5, pp. 357-80. (*Maréchal Reader,* pp. 161-66.)

22. *Le Point de Départ,* v. 5, pp. 317-19. (*Maréchal Reader,* pp. 153-54.)

23. *Le Point de Départ,* v. 5, pp. 346-55. (*Maréchal Reader,* pp. 154-61.)

24. The transcendental critique of the object is found on pp. 505-60 of the fifth volume. (*Maréchal Reader,* pp. 217-31.)

25. *Le Point de Départ,* v. 5, pp. 532-60. (*Maréchal Reader,* pp. 221-29.)

26. *Le Point de Départ,* v. 5, pp. 516-19. (*Maréchal Reader,* pp. 217-18.)

27. *Le Point de Départ,* v. 5, pp. 530-38. (*Maréchal Reader,* pp. 220-22.)

28. *Le Point de Départ,* v. 5, pp. 554-55. (*Maréchal Reader,* p. 223.)

29. For an excellent account of Maréchal's epistemology see Van Riet, *L'Epistémologie Thomiste,* pp. 263-300. See also the more recent article by Johannes B. Lotz, S.J., "Joseph Maréchal" in E. Coreth, *Christliche Philosophie im katholischen Denken,* v. 2, pp. 453-69. In addition to its expository value Lotz's article contains a very useful and well chosen bibliography.

30. *L'Intellectualisme de Saint Thomas,* p. v.

Chapter Seven
Thomism and History: Étienne Gilson

From its early days in the nineteenth century the Neo-Thomist movement had directed its attention to the historical study of its mediæval heritage. Promoting the study of mediæval history and encouraging the recovery of mediæval texts and their careful editing had been part of the movement's agenda practically from its start. Beginning with the work of Denifle (1844-1905) and Ehrle (1845-1934) and with the editing of the works of Thomas and Bonaventure in the nineteenth century, organized research into the historical sources of mediæval philosophy had grown steadily in its quality and importance during the twentieth. Martin Grabmann (1875-1949) carried on the tradition of textual study which Clemens Bäumker (1853-1924) had established solidly in Germany. Maurice De Wulf (1867-1947), one of Mercier's first team of professors at Louvain, had made the study of mediæval philosophy one of the central elements of the philosophy program there, and, as other distinguished historians, such as Fernand Van Steenberghen (1904-93), succeeded De Wulf in the Chair of Mediæval Philosophy, Louvain retained its importance as a center for mediæval studies.

Complementing the Dominican tradition of systematic Thomism, which Ambroise Gardeil had established at Le Saulchoir, there was a Dominican historical tradition as well, which went back to Pierre Mandonnet. This was the scholarly tradition from which the remarkable historical work of Marie-Dominique Chenu would emerge later in the century; and the mid-century clash between the historically orientated Thomism of Chenu and the systematically oriented Thomism of Garrigou-Lagrange was a particularly dramatic example of the effect which the growth in its historical understanding of the middle ages had upon the interpretation of St. Thomas's own philosophy within the Neo-Thomistic movement.

The philosopher who best exemplified the interplay between historical research and speculative development in Neo-Thomism was Étienne Gilson (1884-1978). Gilson may well have been the most influential historian of mediæval philosophy within the movement and, on the basis of his textual research, he originated the important speculative school of Neo-Thomism called "existential Thomism."[1]

As doggedly independent in his philosophical thinking as he was firm in his religious commitment to the Catholic faith, Gilson had discovered Thomism on his own. He owed no allegiance to any of the traditional schools in his interpretation of St. Thomas's text. The field of Gilson's professional interest as a graduate student at the Sorbonne had been Cartesian and post-Cartesian philosophy and his first contact with mediæval philosophy had come from a suggestion by his mentor, Lucien Lévy-Bruhl (1857-1939), that the Scholastic origins of Descartes's thought could be a very good topic for his doctoral dissertation. It was. The doctoral dissertation was *La Liberté chez Descartes et la Théologie*, and by the time that it was published in 1913 Gilson had made himself a first class mediævalist.[2]

His reputation as a philosopher grew rapidly and during the first half of the twentieth century he was often invited to lecture in Europe and America. Two of his lectures, the Gifford Lectures at Aberdeen, and the William James Lectures at Harvard were published as two of Gilson's most widely read books, *The Spirit of Mediæval Philosophy* and *The Unity of Philosophical Experience*.[3] Gilson was appointed to the professorship of Mediæval Philosophy at the Sorbonne in 1921 and to the Chair of Mediæval Studies at the Collège de France in 1932. In 1929 he was invited to found the Institute of Mediæval Studies at the University of Toronto which received its Pontifical Charter in 1939. In 1951 Gilson resigned his chair at the Collège de France to devote all his energies to his work at Toronto. As the Institute flourished, a steady flow of highly trained and devoted students carried Gilson's approach to Thomism to all parts of North America.

Christian Philosophy as the Spirit of Mediæval Philosophy.

His study of Descartes's mediæval antecedents made it clear to Gilson that the conception of mediæval philosophy then current in university circles was erroneous.[4] It had been simply taken for granted that philosophy began again in the seventeenth century at the point where ancient philosophy had ended. Nothing of philosophical consequence had occurred in the interval. But Descartes's proven dependence on the mediæval theologians showed that this could not be true. Descartes's infinite subsistent God, the omnipotent, free Creator, who grounded the being of the world through His efficient causality, was a stranger to the thought of Plato and Aristotle. Descartes's immortal man was not the mortal man of Aristotle. Indeed, neither the God nor the man who appeared in the systems of Descartes (1596-1650), Leibnitz (1646-1716), or Spinoza (1632-77), appeared in the finite, self-grounding world of the Greek philosophers. Yet they were omnipresent in the philosophical theology of the mediæval Doctors. Evidently then philosophy had undergone a remarkable development through its contact with Christian faith in mediæval theology; and that development had expanded and enriched it. It was this developed philosophy—and not the philosophy of the Greeks—which the seventeenth century rationalists had taken over, whether they realized it or not.[5] There was such a thing then as the history of mediæval philosophy, and it would be worth their while for modern philosophers to study it.

Contact between Greek metaphysics and Christian revelation in the believing minds of the mediæval theologians had proven to be the source of a profound and authentic development for philosophy. It was this contact in fact which accounted for the uniqueness, originality, and vigor which Gilson's research had discovered in mediæval metaphysics. Philosophy in the Middle Ages was a living element in the theology of the mediæval Doctors; but it did not cease to be genuine philosophy because it was carried on in a theological context. On the contrary, the rigor of its reflection was enhanced and the range of its vision was enlarged.[6]

Descartes and his modern successors, on the other hand, methodically separated their philosophy from the context of faith and revelation. Pre-Christian Greek philosophy knew nothing about either. Therefore, both modern and Greek philosophy could be considered "separate philosophies" whereas mediæval philosophy, inserted as it was into the context of a living theology, should be more properly called a Christian philosophy.[7] Christian philosophy therefore, in the sense which Gilson gave the term, was not intended to be the name of a philosophical system. It was meant to designate *a special way of doing philosophy*, i.e. the way in which the mediæval theologians did it.[8] That way of "philosophizing inside theology," common to all the mediæval Doctors, constituted what Gilson called *the spirit of mediæval philosophy*.[9]

The Context, Sources, and Order of Christian Philosophy.

Since mediæval philosophy was a Christian philosophy, Gilson believed that its history must be studied from a theological perspective rather than from a strictly philosophical one. When mediæval philosophy was studied from a philosophical perspective its history focussed on Aristotle's commentators, especially Averroes, and their role in the emergence of an independent philosophy. But, if mediæval philosophy was studied from this viewpoint, its originality could easily be overlooked. It might indeed be reduced to a mediæval variety of Aristotelianism. The creative thinkers in the Middle Ages had not been Aristotle's commentators. They had been the Christian theologians; and the historian who hoped to bring the originality of their distinctive philosophies to light would have to study them from a theological perspective.[10]

That significant change in perspective in the study of mediæval philosophy had important consequences for Gilson's own interpretation of St. Thomas. St. Thomas's original and authentic philosophy, Gilson believed, must be derived *exclusively from the Angelic Doctor's theological works*.[11] Other Neo-Thomists, following the example of Thomas's seventeenth century commentators, continued to base their interpretation of his philosophy on *both the philosophical and the theological works* of the Angelic Doctor, particularly St. Thomas's commentaries on Aristotle. By refusing to accept even St. Thomas's own commentaries on Aristotle as valid sources of the Angelic Doctor's authentic philosophy, Gilson was laying down a strict methodological principle for the exegesis of St. Thomas. The Christian philosophy of St. Thomas must be rigidly confined to the philosophy contained in the purely theological works of the Angelic Doctor.

On the basis of his own understanding of Christian philosophy, Gilson also took issue with the Thomism found in the seventeenth and eighteenth century philosophical manuals. Reacting to the challenge of Descartes's modern philosophy, these manuals organized their "theses," excerpted from the works of the Angelic Doctor, in the form of a rival "separate" philosophy. Thomism then ceased to operate within the context of theology. Like the other "separate" philosophies, it argued from the world to God, following the ascending order of philosophy. Once these changes had been made, Gilson said flatly, the philosophy presented in these Thomistic manuals, could no longer be called the authentic Christian philosophy of the Angelic Doctor.[12] Since Christian philosophy was carried on inside the context of theology, the order of its exposition must be theological as well. In other words, its philosophical exposition must descend from God to the world, following the order of the *Summa Theologiae*. It could not ascend from the world to God in the philosophical order of the modern systems. Thus, in the more restricted range of its accepted sources, in its theological context, and in the required theological order of its exposition, Gilsonian Thomism distinguished itself clearly from the philosophies of the other Neo-Thomists.

The Pluralism of Mediæval Philosophy.

By shifting the focus of the history of mediæval philosophy from a philosophical to a theological perspective, Gilson was able to bring to light, through his studies on St. Bonaventure, St. Augustine, St. Thomas, and Duns Scotus, the radical differences in the metaphysics which structured their theologies.[13] Once again, historical research was leading to a revision in Thomism's understanding its own nature. At the beginning of the Neo-Scholastic revival, Leo XIII's Encyclical, *Aeterni Patris*, had praised the philosophy of St. Thomas as the finest example of the philosophy "common to all the Scholastic Doctors." The editors of the Quaracchi edition of St. Bonaventure had taken pains to point out the similarities which could be found between the philosophies of St. Bonaventure and St. Thomas. In the earlier editions of his *History of Mediæval Philosophy*, the distinguished Louvain historian, Maurice De Wulf, had argued for the existence of a common scholastic synthesis derived from the Aristotelian form of thought which all the Scholastic Doctors shared.

On the basis of his own research, however, Gilson concluded that nothing like a common scholastic synthesis had existed. The unity of mediæval philosophy was not therefore a unity of systematic content. It was a "unity of spirit." In other words, it was a unity based on the way of philosophizing inside theology which all of the scholastic Doctors shared. For, despite their "unity of spirit," the philosophies of knowledge, man, and being found in the theologies of St. Thomas, St. Bonaventure, and Duns Scotus were irreducibly distinct in their systematic content. In their proofs for God's existence, in the role assigned to the divine ideas in human knowledge, in their approach to the analogy of being, and in their adaptation of Aristotelian act and potency, radical differences could be found in these philosophies. Thomism consequently could not be simply a more developed form of a common scholastic Aristotelianism. Thomism was a unique and original system of philosophy, distinct both from the philosophy of Aristotle and from the philosophies of the other scholastic Doctors.

Augustine's Platonic Metaphysics of Being.

In Augustine's Christian Platonism, Plotinus's metaphysics of the good had been transposed into a metaphysics of being. For once Augustine had learned from the Book of Exodus that the name of God was "I am Who am," he realized that the primary source of all reality had to be self-grounding being. It could not be the Infinite One of Plotinus, the Primal Good, which was not being, and from which the finite world of beings flowed by necessary emanation. On the contrary, the ground and source of all reality had to be the eternal changeless being of its Infinite Creator, and the finite world proceeding from that source had to be a created universe of temporal beings, whose contingent nature made them a mutable blend of being and non-being. The primal division in reality was no longer the cleft between the Infinite Good and finite beings; it was the chasm between necessary and contingent being. In Augustine's Christian philosophy, God knew the world eternally through His own divine ideas and produced its temporal dependent being through His free act of creation.[14]

Christian convert though the was, Augustine never ceased to be a Platonist. Like Plato's man, Augustinian man was identified with the human soul, linked loosely to its body. For Augustine sensation was an operation of the soul alone, as it had been for Plato. It was not a cooperative activity of soul and body, as it had been for Aristotle, and as it would be for Thomas. Without its "recollection" of the Form's changeless intelligibility, no Platonic mind could make a stable judgment, and neither could the contingent and unstable mind of an Augustinian knower without its "memory" of God's "changeless truth" in the "light above it." For its mysterious contact with the eternal world of the divine ideas, through the process of "divine illumination," was the source of the increase in its power which enabled a contingent mind to make true judgments under the necessary laws of being.[15]

Christian through its contact with revelation, Augustine's philosophy was still Platonic through the definition of being which it had inherited from Plato. Being was understood in terms of changeless intelligibility, the immutable truth, which Plato had attributed to his eternal essences or Forms, and which Augustine had attributed to the abiding intelligibility of the God who eternally remained what He was. One of the great difficulties with the Platonic metaphysics, in which being is defined in terms of necessary, changeless truth, is that the contingent mutable existents of our temporal world scarcely deserve the name of being.[16] And, in Augustinianism, this definition of being led to what Gilson considered one of the great defects of its metaphysics, its inability to grant their proper autonomy to the contingent beings and agents of our finite world.[17] That deficiency revealed itself most clearly through Augustine's demand for "divine illumination" as the condition of possibility for human knowledge.[18] But it revealed itself as well in the Augustinian account of physical change. Every new form produced in change must have been virtually contained in its preexisting "seminal reason." For contingent mutable agents, since they lacked full reality themselves, could not have the power to produce real change in others which autonomous finite agents all possessed in St. Thomas's philosophy of being.[19]

Thomas's Metaphysics of Existence.

Thomas was closer to Aristotle than he was to Plato. That did not mean however, as a number of Neo-Thomists seemed to think, that the decisive difference between his Christian philosophy and the Christian philosophy of St. Augustine should be attributed to Thomas's commitment to the Aristotelian metaphysics of substance, act, and potency.[20] If that were the case, Thomism would be in its essence a Christianized version of Aristotle's philosophy of being. That was impossible, Gilson argued, since his own research had shown that the metaphysics of Thomas and the metaphysics of Aristotle were irreducibly distinct. The reason for their unbridgeable diversity was found in the diverse definitions which they gave to being in their philosophies. Being for Aristotle meant substance, the concrete subsisting essence, whether that subsisting essence was a pure substantial form or a composite of substantial form and primary matter.[21] For Thomas, on the other hand, being meant existence, an act which could not be a form, since its function was to confer its actual existence on the already formed essence which received it.[22]

Consequently, in St. Thomas's philosophy of knowledge, being could not be known, in the manner of an Aristotelian form, through a process of abstraction. It could be known only through the judgment, the act of knowledge which affirmed the actual existence of a corporeal reality manifested to the human knower through his sense experience.[23] Therefore, the metaphysics of St. Thomas was neither a Platonic metaphysics of form or an Aristotelian metaphysics of substance; it was the distinctive form of metaphysics, found in the Christian philosophy of St. Thomas alone, the Thomistic metaphysics of existence.

When Thomas discovered the name of God in the Book of Exodus, he realized that "I am Who Am" was meant to indicate that the distinguishing mark of God was His pure and unlimited existence. This "sublime truth" of Christian revelation meant that, although God was indeed Pure Act, that Pure Act could not be a Substantial Form, as it was in the metaphysics of Aristotle. It could only be a Pure Act of Existence. [23a] Therefore, the reality which God communicated to His creatures through the creative activity of His efficient causality had to be the fundamental act of *existence*. Hence the perfection which the finite participants in God's reality communicated to their fellow creatures through their own efficient causality must also be the perfection of existence. For Thomas then to be real and intelligible meant to exist, and to exercise efficient causality meant *to communicate existence*. As Thomas himself put it, *agere sequitur esse* (action follows from existence).[24]

That discovery transformed the whole Christian philosophy of St. Thomas. His philosophy of being and its attributes, his metaphysics of creation and causality, his philosophy of man and his philosophy of knowledge were different from their counterparts in every other Christian philosophy because in Thomism alone to be meant to exist. Gilson's extended analysis of the Thomistic proofs for God's existence and of Thomas's metaphysics of God's attributes were clearly intended to prove that point. So also was Gilson's detailed discussion of a decisive point in favor of his thesis, St. Thomas's philosophical proof for the soul's immortality. Why, he asked, did Thomas attempt to make such a proof when most Christian philosophers, including his own great commentator, Cajetan, did not believe that it was possible to do so? The only reason could be, Gilson replied, that, for Thomas, to be meant to exist. In his existential metaphysics the act of existence which the spiritual soul communicated to the matter of its body already belonged to it, by priority of nature, as its own proper act of being. It was because the spiritually subsisting soul was already placed in being through its own proper act of existence that it could continue to exist after its separation from the body. In other words, the real distinction between essence and existence, demanded by St. Thomas's definition of being, was required for the validity of his proof.[25] That was why St. Thomas alone could offer it whereas other Christian philosophers could not. There could be no question then that the metaphysics of being, which structured the Christian philosophy of St. Thomas, was the distinctive Thomistic metaphysics of existence.

Scotus's Metaphysics of Possible Being.

Thomas's Christian philosophy therefore, as a metaphysics of existence, distinguished itself from the metaphysics of the Franciscan Doctors. As we have seen, Gilson had argued in *The Philosophy of St. Bonaventure* that the greatest among the Doctors of the early Franciscan School had worked out his own Christian philosophy in deliberate opposition to the Christian philosophy of the Angelic Doctor.[26] Later on in his career, Gilson undertook an in-depth study of Duns Scotus in his *Jean Duns Scot.* Different though the premier Doctor of the late Franciscan School had been from Bonaventure in his Christian philosophy, the difference between Scotus and Aquinas was even greater. Once again, the diversity between the two Christian philosophers could be traced back to their disagreement over the meaning of being.

Scotus had created his own metaphysics as an explicit response to the Greek necessitarianism of Avicenna. Avicenna's world of finite essences emanated with iron necessity from its infinite first principle, and, in that process, free creation played no part. To counter Avicenna's threat to Christian faith, Scotus worked out a metaphysics of necessary and possible being. Nevertheless, he accepted Avicenna's conception of essence as his own.[27] Every essence had its own intrinsic intelligibility, to which actual existence, in the intramental or extra-mental order, was no more than an accidental addition. And so the intelligible reality of an essence was independent of its actual existence.

In the metaphysics of Avicenna, finite essences, contingent in their own reality, owed their actual existence to their necessary emanation from the Infinite First Being. In order to refute that thesis, Scotus proposed, as an alternative, his own metaphysics of possible being. No essence, even though it was known to God through His divine ideas, could be real in itself, in the sense of being intrinsically possible. Possibility was conferred upon an essence by an absolutely free decision of God's will which selected it as a possible object for His own act of creation. Therefore every essence, except God's own, was radically contingent in its very possibility.[28]

Scotus's world of essences then was divided into the necessary essence of God, the infinite ground of all possibility, and the radically contingent essences whose very possibility depended upon God's absolutely free choice.[29] Thus, the possibility of an essence, rather than its actual existence, became the decisive element in Scotus's philosophy of being. Existence in fact was considered no more than a mode which brought a possible essence to its fully constituted state of extra-mental reality. Furthermore, in such an existing essence, every intrinsic formality representable in an idea must have an "essential reality" of its own. This meant, Gilson explained, that even the famous Scotistic "plurality of substantial forms," through which the diverse specific forms which made up the completed substance were distinguished from each other by Scotus's "real formal distinction," was simply a further demand of his metaphysics of possible being.[30]

These were not the only differences with the Christian philosophy of St. Thomas required by the same metaphysics. The Scotistic proofs for God's existence as the infinite and necessary ground of *every finite essence's possibility* were completely different from Thomas's proofs for God's existence as the efficient cause of a possible essence's *actual existence* or the final cause of its contingent motion.[31] The account which Scotus gave of the analogy of being could not be the same as the one which Thomas gave, since their metaphysics of essence and existence were completely different.[32] The demands of Scotus's "real formal distinction" made his metaphysics of God's attributes radically different from the Thomistic metaphysics of God's being.[33] And, given the differences which we have already seen in their metaphysics, the philosophies of man and knowledge proposed by these two Christian philosophers had to be as diverse as their philosophies of God had been.

Both Christian philosophies, it was true, were structured by a metaphysics of being, and the same could be said of the Christian philosophy of St. Augustine. Nevertheless, each of these three philosophers had proposed a different explanation of what it meant to be. For Augustine, being meant "changeless truth"; for Thomas, it meant "the act of existence"; and, for Scotus, it meant "possible essence." From these diverse definitions of being had come their radically diverse systems of metaphysics. Although all its Christian philosophers were united in their "spirit" through the common way in which they philosophized, there could be no systematic unity in their Christian philosophies. The reason was that they had failed to reach agreement on what it meant to be.

The Only Authentic Thomism.

Gilson concluded on the basis of his own historical research that the only authentic Thomism was the Christian philosophy which he had discovered in the theological works of the Angelic Doctor. Certainly Suarezianism was not authentic Thomism. For, despite Francis Suárez's profession of fidelity to St. Thomas, the definition of being in his metaphysics was not the definition of Aquinas. Being for Suárez no longer meant "existence." On the contrary, it meant "essence." It meant "essence" too in the metaphysics of nineteenth century Jesuit Neo-Scholastics, such as Joseph Kleutgen.[34] For that reason their Suarezian philosophy of man and being did not agree with the philosophy of Aquinas himself. Infidelity to St. Thomas could also be found in the Dominican Thomism, inherited from St. Thomas's great commentators through the manuals of the seventeenth and the eighteenth centuries. The "separated" philosophy presented in those manuals, arguing as it did in the ascending order which rose from the world to God, had ceased to be the Christian philosophy of St. Thomas. St. Thomas's own philosophy was always found in the context of theology and its exposition followed theology's descending order from God to the world.

Furthermore, not even the great commentators themselves had been faithful enough in their interpretation of St. Thomas. Cajetan, as Gilson had shown, had failed to grasp the essential role of the act of existence in St. Thomas's own philosophy of man; and the Cajetanian epistemology of the three degrees of conceptual abstraction—upon which Maritain had built *The Degrees of Knowledge*—was evidence that Cajetan had also failed to realize that the affirmation of the judgment—and not the abstraction of the concept—was the only source through which the unique intelligibility of existence could be grasped and "separated" from the quite diverse intelligibility of essence.

Gilson was even more forceful in his dismissal of Maréchalian Thomism. Maréchal, in his opinion, had never really understood the philosophy of either Kant or Thomas.

Thomas had defended a frank realism because he had realized that being can only be grasped through the mind's existential judgments about the objects of direct sense experience. Once the mind encloses itself—even "precisively"—in
consciousness and severs its immediate link with sensible
reality, contact with real being can never be restored. There
was nothing inconsistent then about Kant's remaining an idealist. Any attempt to accept Kant's starting point in order to
work one's way out of consciousness to real being proved
nothing except that its author had failed to understand the
necessary implications of Kant's transcendental method.
There was nothing to be gained by these endeavors to bring
Thomism up to date by adopting the starting point and
method of modern idealistic systems.[35] Study of St. Thomas
and his disciples led to only one conclusion. The way to be a
genuine Thomist was to philosophize in the way in which
St. Thomas himself had done. There was only one authentic
Thomist, St. Thomas himself.[36]

The Influence of History on Neo-Thomism.

Not all historians of philosophy and theology accepted
Gilson's interpretation of Christian philosophy without reserve. The distinguished Louvain mediævalist, Fernand Van
Steenberghen (1904-93), for example, denied vigorously that
any coherent philosophy of that sort could be found in the
works of St. Bonaventure.[37] James Collins, a Thomist historian of modern philosophy, rejected Gilson's claim that authentic Thomism must follow the descending order of theology.[38] Other Thomists, Henri de Lubac and Henri Bouillard
among them, showed more sympathy to the Thomism of
Rousselot and Maréchal as the result of their historical research than they did to the existential Thomism of Gilson.

Nevertheless the research of de Lubac and Bouillard
supported Gilson's claim that the great Dominican commentators had not been faithful interpreters of the Angelic Doctor. In his *Surnaturel*, de Lubac had shown that the theology
of nature and grace which Cajetan had attributed to St. Thomas, and which Suárez also accepted, was not St. Thomas's

own theology.[39] Therefore in their theology of grace neither Suárezianism nor the Thomism of the commentators deserved the name of authentic Thomism. This meant that the two great traditions of the Second Scholasticism could no longer serve as unquestioned norms of Thomistic orthodoxy. History had to assume the role of determining what Thomas really taught.

This change of perspective manifested itself dramatically at the Dominican House of Studies at Le Saulchoir. Marie-Dominique Chenu, who had become the Regent of Studies there, was an outstanding historian of mediæval theology. His studies on the theologies of the twelfth and thirteenth centuries, his treaties on the theology of faith, and his introduction to St. Thomas have all become classics.[40] Like Gilson, Chenu believed that the teaching of St. Thomas should be guided by historical study of his text rather than by the works of Thomas's great commentators, and, in 1942, he proposed that the course of studies at Le Saulchoir be revised along those lines. The reaction from Rome, where the influence of Garrigou-Lagrange was strong, was negative, and Chenu found himself removed from his position.[41]

Official discouragement did not however prevent the historical tradition of Mandonnet from flourishing in the Order of Preachers, and the subsequent historical work of Dominicans, like Daniel Callus, Ignatius Eschmann, and James Weisheipl are evidence of that.[42]

Another result of the historical study of St. Thomas was the rediscovery of the central role which Platonic participation metaphysics had played in his philosophy. Two of the pioneering studies to which the rediscovery was due were *La Participation dans la Philosophie de S. Thomas* by the Dominican Thomist, L.B. Geiger and *La Nozione Metafisica di Participazione* by Cornelio Fabro.[43] The impact of their historical research on the speculative development of Thomism could be seen in *The Philosophy of Being* by the Louvain metaphysician, Louis De Raeymaeker, and *L'Être et l'Agir dans la Philosophie de Saint Thomas*, another well known Thomist who taught at the Jesuit Gregorian University at Rome.[44]

The distinction between the Thomism of St. Thomas and the Thomism of his commentators, which the historians had made it impossible to deny, made it harder for the representatives of any of the traditional "schools" to claim, as they had in the past, that their interpretation of Aquinas should be taken as the "authentic" one. Yet, since the historians also disagreed with one another, as did Gilson and Van Steenberghen, even the "historical St. Thomas" might bear the fingerprints of his historical "discoverers." Thomism, and the determination of its "authenticity" was becoming more a matter of independent judgment than of commitment to a "tradition" or a "movement."

Notes

1. The best source for information about Gilson is the masterly biography by Laurence K. Shook, C.S.B., *Étienne Gilson* (Toronto: The Pontifical Institute of Mediæval Studies, 1984). An account of Gilson's epistemology can be found in Van Riet, *L'Epistémologie Thomiste*, pp. 495-517. For a fine and more recent account of Gilson's philosophy see Armand Maurer, C.S.B., "Étienne Gilson," in *Christliche Philosophie im katholischen Denken*, v. 2, pp. 519-45. See also Maurer's "The Legacy of Étienne Gilson," in Victor B. Brezik, C.S.B., ed., *One Hundred Years of Thomism* (Houston: University of St. Thomas, 1981).

2. *La Liberté chez Descartes et la Théologie* (Paris: Alcan, 1913).

3. *The Spirit of Mediæval Philosophy* (New York: Scribner's, 1940). *The Unity of Philosophical Experience* (New York: Scribner's, 1937).

4. *The Philosopher and Theology* (New York: Random House, 1962), pp. 88-91.

5. *The Philosopher and Theology*, pp. 89 -90.

6. See "What Is Christian Philosophy?" in Anton C. Pegis, ed., *A Gilson Reader* (Garden City: Doubleday-Image, 1957), pp. 177-91.

7. "What Is Christian Philosophy?," pp. 183-94.

8. *The Philosopher and Theology*, pp. 189-94.

9. *The Spirit of Mediæval Philosophy*, pp. 403-26.

10. *The History of Christian Philosophy in the Middle Ages* (New York: Random House, 1955), pp. 540-45.

11. *The Philosopher and Theology*, p. 91.

12. "What Is Christian Philosophy?," pp. 183-85.

13. *The Philosophy of St. Bonaventure* (New York: Sheed & Ward, 1938). *The Christian Philosophy of St. Thomas Aquinas* (New York: Random House, 1956). *Elements of Christian Philosophy* (Garden City: Doubleday, 1957). *The Christian Philosophy of Saint Augustine* (New York: Random House, 1960). *Jean Duns Scot: Introduction à Ses Positions Fondamentales* (Paris: Vrin, 1952).

14. "God and Christian Philosophy" in *God and Philosophy* (New Haven: Yale University Press, 1941), pp. 38-73, esp. pp. 45-61.

15. *The Christian Philosophy of Saint Augustine*, pp. 87-91.

16. *The Spirit of Mediæval Philosophy*, pp. 130-34.

17. *The Spirit of Mediæval Philosophy*, pp. 144-47.

18. *The Spirit of Mediæval Philosophy*, pp. 135-39.

19. *The Spirit of Mediæval Philosophy*, pp. 134-36.

20. This was the thesis defended by Gallus Manser, O.P. in *Das Wesen des Thomismus* (Freiburg in der Schweiz: Paulusverlag, 1949).

21. *Being and Some Philosophers* (Toronto: Pontifical Institute of Mediæval Studies, 1952, pp. 41-73.

22. *Being and Some Philosophers*, pp. 154-89.

23. *Elements of Christian Philosophy*, pp. 225-35. *Being and Some Philosophers*, pp. 190-205.

23a. *The Christian Philosophy of St. Thomas Aquinas*, pp. 84-95.

24. *Elements of Christian Philosophy*, pp. 184-202.

25. *Elements of Christian Philosophy*, pp. 210-19. Another example of the failure of the great commentators to understand the true nature of St. Thomas's metaphysics of existence was Bañez's assertion that accidents had their own act of existence. *The Christian Philosophy of St. Thomas Aquinas*, pp. vii-viii.

26. *The Philosophy of Saint Bonaventure*, pp. 470-95.

27. *Being and Some Philosophers*, pp. 84-86.

28. *Being and Some Philosophers*, pp. 85-87.

29. *Jean Duns Scot*, pp. 318-28.

30. *Being and Some Philosophers*, pp. 88-89. *Jean Duns Scot*, pp. 492-97.

31. *Jean Duns Scot*, pp. 177-215.

32. *Jean Duns Scot*, pp. 84-115.

33. *Jean Duns Scot*, pp. 243-54.

34. *Being and Some Philosophers*, pp. 96-120.

35. *Thomist Realism and the Critique of Knowledge* (San Francisco: Ignatius Press, 1986), pp. 129-48.

36. *The Philosopher and Theology*, pp. 200-14.

37. Fernand Van Steenberghen, *The Philosophical Movement in the Thirteenth Century* (Edinburgh: Nelson, 1955), pp. 56-74.

38. James Collins, *Three Paths in Philosophy* (Chicago: Regnery, 1962), pp. 280-99.

39. Henri de Lubac, S.J., *Surnaturel: Études Historiques* (Paris: Aubier, 1946), pp. 105-16.

40. *Theology in the Twelfth Century* (Chicago: University of Chicago Press, 1968), *La Théologie comme Science au XIIIe Siècle* (Paris: Vrin, 1957), *Faith and Theology* (New York: Macmillan, 1968).

41. Chenu's plan of studies with more recent reactions of a number of theologians to it can be found in Chenu's *Une École de Théologie: Le Saulchoir* (Paris: Cerf, 1985).

42. See James A. Weisheipl, O.P., *Friar Thomas D'Aquino* (Garden City: Doubleday, 1974).

43. L. B. Geiger, O.P., *La Participation dans la Philosophie de S. Thomas d'Aquin* (Turin: Società Editrice Internazionale, 1950).

44. Louis De Raeymaeker, *The Philosophy of Being: A Synthesis of Metaphysics* (St. Louis: B. Herder, 1954). Joseph de Finance, S.J., *Être et Agir dans la Philosophie de Saint Thomas* (Paris: Beauchesne, 1945).

Epilogue

By the middle of the twentieth century Neo-Thomism was a solidly established movement in Catholic philosophy and theology. The organized research into mediæval philosophy and theology, which the Thomistic revival had stimulated, was being carried on in Belgium, France, Germany, and Italy. On the other side of the Atlantic, the Pontifical Institute of Mediæval Studies, which Gilson had established at Toronto in 1929, became a center of historical and textual research from which a steady stream of well-trained philosophers and mediævalists carried the Gilsonian approach to Thomism to the whole North American continent. By the end of the First World War a large and influential system of Catholic colleges and universities had been set up in the United States and Canada. An important place was assigned to philosophy in their liberal arts curriculum, and the professors employed to teach that discipline were Thomistic, or at least Neo-Scholastic, in their orientation. For the first three decades of the century, these North American Thomists received their professional formation at the Catholic University of America or, more frequently, either in the ecclesiastic faculties maintained by the religious orders or in one of the Catholic universities in Europe.

By the end of the Second World War, however, North American universities had begun to play the major role in the education of Catholic teachers of philosophy. Toronto, Laval, Notre Dame, Saint Louis, Marquette, and Fordham, together with the Catholic University of America, became the graduate faculties at which the professors for the hundreds of smaller Catholic colleges were prepared. But European influence remained an important force in North American Thomism, Louvain, the Roman universities, and the

Institut Catholique de Paris still attracted North American students, and prominent European Thomists, such as Étienne Gilson, Jacques Maritain, Yves Simon (1903-61) and Charles de Koninck (1906-65) were invited to teach and lecture in North America. From these varied sources the European Thomisms of Louvain, Gilson, Maritain, and Maréchal were transmitted to thousands of undergraduates in the United States and Canada.[1]

In Europe, Louvain retained its position as a leading center of mediæval research, and the University continued to be the home of a vigorous group of independent Thomists. Louis Noël (1878-1953) and Georges Van Riet (b. 1916) enjoyed high reputations both in Europe and America for their work in epistemology. Nicholas Balthasar, Louis De Raeymaeker (1895-1970), and Fernand Van Steenberghen (1904-93) — who was also an outstanding mediævalist — were equally well appreciated for their work in metaphysics. Jacques Leclercq (1891-1971) made his name as one of Europe's leading experts in Thomistic ethics. Albert Dondeyne (1901-85) extended the range of Thomistic thought through his dialogue with the phenomenology and existentialism whose influence at Louvain began to grow after the Second World War.[2]

New currents manifested themselves near the middle of the century in the flourishing European Neo-Thomism. One of them was a stress on the role that should be assigned to Platonic participation metaphysics in the philosophy of the Angelic Doctor. Historical research, notably the textual studies of Louis Geiger (b. 1906) and Cornelio Fabro (b. 1911) had called the attention of students of St. Thomas to the significance his Platonic participation metaphysics.[3] As a result, instead of being considered a Christian form of Aristotelianism, as it had been in the past, or as a sound reaction against the excesses of Platonism, as Gilson was inclined to view it, Thomism began to be presented as a metaphysics of existence in which the structure of its finite participants was determined through St. Thomas's transposition of the participation metaphysics which he had inherited from Plato.

The influence of this historical research into St. Thomas's use of participation metaphysics soon showed itself in the systematic Thomism of his European followers. It could be found, for instance, in the Louvain Thomism of Louis De Raeymaeker, in the Maréchalian Thomism of Joseph de Finance (b. 1904), in the independent Thomism of the Irish Jesuit, Arthur Little, and in the systematic philosophy of Cornelio Fabro.[4] Another important development in mid-century Thomism was the rediscovery of a distinctive metaphysics of the person and of interpersonal relations in the philosophy of St. Thomas. Maritain had already given a good deal of attention to St. Thomas's metaphysics of the person, and the attraction which the Christian personalism of Gabriel Marcel exercised on Catholic intellectuals in the early postwar years helped to stimulate the growing interest in St. Thomas's philosophy of the person among his European disciples. Thomistic personalism would remain an important force in Catholic thought for the rest of the century. In North America it would be exploited by the independent Thomist, William Norris Clarke (b. 1915), and, in Poland, as is well known, one of its leading exponents would be Karol Wojtila (b. 1920), the present Pope John Paul II.

The End of the Unified Neo-Thomist Movement.

In the second half of the twentieth century, however, Neo-Thomism no longer held the dominant position which it had acquired in Catholic thought after the publication of Leo XIII's *Aeterni Patris*. It became more difficult for Neo-Thomists themselves to look on their philosophical theology as the changeless unified system which he nineteenth century Scholastics had taken it to be. Their own historical research into the philosophy and theology of St. Thomas himself and of the great Dominican and Jesuit theologians of the Second Scholasticism, for example, had made it clear that the systems defended by Thomas's disciples in the sixteenth and seventeenth centuries could no longer be presented as identical, in their essentials at least, with the thought of the Angelic Doctor. Suarezianism and Thomism were generally admitted to be distinct philosophies. Gilson and other historians had proven that, in their philosophy of knowledge and being, two of the great Dominican Thomists, Cajetan and Bañez, had deviated from the teaching of St. Thomas himself. Henri de Lubac had established that the sixteenth century Scholastic theology of nature and grace, first introduced by Cajetan and then taken up by Suárez, differed markedly from the theology of grace and nature which St. Thomas himself had defended. Tension became inevitable then between the "way of being a Thomist" advocated by his historically minded disciples, such as Étienne Gilson, Marie-Dominique Chenu, and Henri de Lubac (b. 1896), and the "fidelity to the tradition of the schools" manifested by staunch Suárezians, like Pedro Descoqs, or "orthodox Thomists," like Réginald Garrigou-Lagrange.

Divergences in their systematic approach to Thomism marked off the different schools within the movement as they established their own identity. Transcendental Thomists, in the tradition of Rousselot and Maréchal, could be clearly distinguished from the adherents of Gilson and Maritain by their use of Kant's Transcendental Method in their Thomistic epistemology. Furthermore, since these Transcendental Thomists grounded the mind's grasp of being on the movement of the mind to God, operative in the judgment, rather than on the abstract concept of being, they came into conflict also with the theologians influenced by the epistemology of Garrigou-Lagrange. For Rousselot, as a Transcendental Thomist, the concept as such as much less important than it was for Garrigou-Lagrange in grounding the absolute and changeless truth of human knowledge required to underpin the Church's dogmatic teaching. Relying on the judgment and the dynamism of the mind to ground the first principles of metaphysics, Rousselot could afford to "relativize" conceptual knowledge, as he did, without fear of falling into "relativism." Garrigou-Lagrange, on the contrary, could not. In his epistemology, "relativizing the concept" would be tantamount to "falling into relativism."

These differences in their approach to St. Thomas ultimately led to serious disputes among the Neo-Thomists themselves. In 1942, as Regent of Studies at Le Saulchoir, Marie-
Dominique Chenu proposed a new plan of studies for the
French Dominican house of formation. Henceforth, St.
Thomas's text would be studied directly, through the historical method, which he and Étienne Gilson employed in
their own writings, rather than through "fidelity to the Dominican Second Scholasticism tradition" in the manner of
Ambroise Gardeil and Réginald Garrigou-Lagrange. Reaction
from Rome, where the influence of Garrigou-Lagrange still
counted, was most unfavorable. Chenu's new plan of studies
was rejected and he himself was removed from office.[5]

Four years later, in 1946, a group of Jesuit Neo-Thomists argued, on the basis of an epistemology influenced by
Rousselot and Maréchal, that, in full fidelity to the teaching
of St. Thomas, they could admit the validity of, at least a
limited, philosophical pluralism. The "relativity" of conceptual knowledge, for which Rousselot had argued in his *Intellectualism of Saint Thomas*, opened the door for a diversity of
logically irreducible frameworks. On the other hand, the
dynamism of every philosopher's mind, operative in the act
of the judgment, secured his hold on being and its immutable first principles, thus preserving him from relativism.
Relativism therefore need not be the inevitable consequence
of a theological pluralism in which the diverse systems of
theology were structured by logically irreducible philosophies.

Garrigou-Lagrange reacted negatively to this Transcendental Thomist vindication of pluralism, as did a number of
other Dominican theologians, who had been influenced by
Maritain's *The Degrees of Knowledge*. Among the fully developed systems of philosophy, as they saw it, Thomism alone
could make the claim to be the true one. Therefore, there
could be no such thing as a theoretically justified pluralism
of fully developed philosophy or theology.[6]

Intervention by Rome brought this debate—which had
become heated—to an abrupt conclusion. Nevertheless, the

pressure within the Church for greater openness toward history in the study of theology and more willingness to allow for pluralism in its systematic structuring continued to build up. Two decades later then, the Second Vatican Council, while admitting the primary place to be accorded to the wisdom of St. Thomas in the formation of the Church's clergy, relaxed the requirement, which Leo XIII had laid down in *Aeterni Patris*, that the philosophy and theology of St. Thomas be used, practically to the exclusion of other systems, in the education of future priests. In that sense then Thomism no longer enjoyed its place of honor as the Church's "official system" and, in the post-Conciliar years, philosophy and theology in the tradition of St. Thomas found themselves in competition with a multitude of other systems.

The Second Vatican Council, and the intellectual ferment which follow it, brought an end to anything like an organized Neo-Thomistic movement. Nevertheless, philosophy and theology in the tradition of St. Thomas remain alive both in Europe and America. In its epistemology and its metaphysics, the philosophical theology of Karl Rahner (1904-84) shows the influence of the Maréchalian Thomism which Rahner studied as a graduate student.[7] Bernard Lonergan's early work was stimulated by the historical and textual research done by Thomists earlier in the century. His two major works, *Insight* and *Method in Theology*, are both built upon the dynamism of the mind familiar to readers of Maréchal, and both of them carry further the exploitation of the role of insight or *intellectus* in human knowledge to which Rousselot had called attention early in this century.[8] Both Rahner and Lonergan were creative and original thinkers whose systems were the result of independent reflection and research. Neither of them wanted to be thought of as a systematic Neo-Thomist. For all of that, however, a good knowledge of the Neo-Thomism, in which both of them were formed, is needed for a proper understanding of their work.

In America, an independent Neo-Thomist, William Norris Clarke, has carried on a lively dialogue with American linguistic philosophers and Whiteheadian process philosophers. Although an American, Clarke received his philosophical formation in Europe and he has incorporated into his own Thomism elements of European participation metaphysics and personalism. From these and from his own reflection he has worked out a Thomistic personalism, in which the prime instantiation of existence, from which it should be studied, as the conscious human person whose essential structure is brought to light through philosophical reflection on concrete interpersonal action. Through his dialogue with process philosophy, Clarke has arrived at an innovative and provocative philosophy of divine knowledge; and he has proposed as well some significant revisions in the Aristotelian metaphysics of relations.[9]

In Poland, the Universities of Cracow and Lublin remain centers of a vital Thomism, still influenced by Gilson and Maritain. Karol Wojtila, who served for years on the faculty at Lublin, proposed in *The Acting Person* a contemporary Thomist metaphysics, whose focus was centered on the individual person, consciously aware of himself as the responsible source of the free actions which bring about his own self-determination. That metaphysics then gave support to Wojtila's Christian ethics, built upon the concrete, self-conscious person, the person's world of values, and the community of persons, rather than on the more abstract universal nature favored by the metaphysical ethics of the earlier Neo-Thomists.[10] In addition to Wojtila, another Thomist well known to the international community of scholars is the Dominican, Mieczyslaw Albert Krapiec (b. 1921) whose Thomism is, in its main lines, at least, an existential Thomism in the tradition of Étienne Gilson.[11]

Despite their links to the earlier Neo-Thomism, to which they all can trace their origin, these Post-Conciliar philosophies and theologies should be considered a new chapter in the history of the tradition of St. Thomas. The organized movement, whose history has been studied in this book, can be said, for all practical purposes, to have reached its end by the time of the Second Vatican Council.

Notes

1. For the history of North American Thomism see Gerald A. McCool, S.J. "The Tradition of St. Thomas in North America: At 50 Years," *The Modern Schoolman* 65 (1988), pp. 185-206.

2. See Jean Ladrière, "Das Löwener Institut in 20 Jahrhundert: F. Van Steenberghen u. a." in *Christliche Philosophie im katholischen Denken*, v. 2, pp. 546-64.

3. Louis B. Geiger, O.P., *La Participation dans la Philosophie de S. Thomas d'Aquin*. (Paris: Vrin, 1953). Cornelio Fabro, *La Nozione Metafisica di Participazione secondo S. Tommaso Di Aquino* (Torino: Società Editrice Internazionale, 1950).

4. Louis De Raeymaeker, *The Philosophy of Being* (St. Louis: B. Herder, 1954). Joseph de Finance, S.J., *Être et Agir dans la Philosophie de Saint Thomas* (Paris: Beauchesne, 1945). Arthur Little, S.J., *The Platonic Heritage of Thomism* (Dublin: Golden Eagle Books, 1949). Cornelio Fabro, *Participation et Causalité selon S. Thomas D'Aquin* (Louvain: Presses Universitaires de Louvain, 1961).

5. See Marie-Dominique Chenu, O.P., *Une École de Théologie: Le Saulchoir* (Paris: Les Editions du Cerf, 1985).

6. For the history of this celebrated controversy, see Gerald A. McCool, S.J., *From Unity to Pluralism: The Internal Evolution of Thomism* (New York: Fordham University Press, 1989), pp. 200-33.

7. For a selection of Rahner's texts and an introduction to his philosophical theology, see Gerald A. McCool, S.J., *A Rahner Reader* (New York: Seabury, 1975).

8. Bernard J.F. Lonergan, S.J., *Insight: A Study in Human Self-Understanding* (New York: Philosophical Library, 1957). *Method in Theology* (New York: Herder & Herder, 1972). For a clear and readable introduction to Lonergan's philosophy, see Hugo A. Meynell, *An Introduction to the Philosophy of Bernard Lonergan* (New York: Barnes and Noble, 1976).

9. See William Norris Clarke, S.J., *The Philosophical Approach to God* (Winston-Salem: Wake Forest University,

1979). For an overview of Clarke's whole system, see Gerald A. McCool, S.J., ed., *The Universe as Journey: Conversations with W. Norris Clarke, S.J.* (New York: Fordham University Press, 1988).

10. Karol Wojtila, *The Acting Person* (Boston: Reidel, 1979). For a general introduction to Wojtila's thought, see Andrew N. Woznicki, *Karol Wojtila's Existential Personalism* (New Britain, CT: Mariel Publications, 1980).

11. For an account of Polish Thomism see Edward Nieznowski, "Polen" in *Christliche Philosophie im Katholischen Denken*, pp. 804-23.

Selected Bibliography
Primary Sources

Blondel, Maurice. *Action: Essay on a Critique of Life and a Science of Practice.* Notre Dame: University of Notre Dame Press, 1984.

_____. *The Letter on Apologetics and History and Dogma.* New York: Holt, Rinehart, and Winston, 1964.

Gardeil, Ambroise. *La Crédibilité et l'Apologétique.* Paris: Gabala, 1908.

_____. *La Structure de l'Ame et l'Expérience Mystique.* Paris: Gabala, 1927.

Garrigou-Lagrange, Reginald. *Reality: A Synthesis of Thomistic Thought.* St. Louis: Herder, 1950.

Gilson, Étienne. *Being and Some Philosophers.* Toronto: The Pontifical Institute of Mediæval Studies, 1952.

_____. *Elements of Christian Philosophy.* Garden City, NY: Doubleday, 1959.

_____. *Thomist Realism and The Critique of Knowledge.* San Francisco: Ignatius Press, 1986.

Maréchal, Joseph. *Le Point de Départ de la Métaphysique. Leçons sur le Développement Historique et Théorique du Problème de la Connaissance.* Paris: Desclée De Brouwer, 1944-49.

_____. *A Maréchal Reader.* Ed. Joseph Donceel, S.J. New York: Herder & Herder, 1970.

Maritain, Jacques. *Creative Intuition in Art and Poetry.* New York: Pantheon, 1955.

_____. *The Degrees of Knowledge.* New York: Scribner's, 1959.

_____. *Existence and the Existent.* New York: Pantheon, 1948.

_____. *Integral Humanism: Temporal and Spiritual Problems*

of a New Humanism. Notre Dame: University of Notre Dame Press, 1973.

_____. *Man and the State*. Chicago: The University of Chicago Press, 1957.

Roland-Gosselin, Marie Dominique. *Essaie d'Une Critique de la Connaissance*. Paris: Vrin, 1932.

Rousselot, Pierre. *The Intellectualism of St. Thomas*. London: Sheed & Ward, 1935.

_____. *The Eyes of Faith*. New York: Fordham University Press, 1990.

Secondary Sources

Aubert, Roger. *Le Problème de l'Acte de Foi*. Louvain: Warny, 1950.

John, Helen James, S.N.D. *The Thomist Spectrum*. New York: Fordham University Press, 1966.

McCool, Gerald A., S.J. *Nineteenth Century Scholasticism: The Search for a Unitary Method*. New York: Fordham University Press, 1989.

Riet, Georges van. *L'Epistémologie Thomiste*. Louvain: Institut Supérieur de Philosophie, 1946.

Coreth, Emerich, Neidl, Walter, Pfligersdorffer, George, eds., *Christliche Philosophie im katholischen Denken des 19. und 20. Jahrhunderts*, v. 2. Graz: Styria, 1988.